[redacted]
W9-BMO-185

Thomas G. Dunn was born and raised in Minnesota. He helped to found and ran the Playwrights' Center of Minnesota for ten years after graduating from the University of Minnesota. During this time he worked for over twenty organizations in Minnesota as a fund-raising consultant. These organizations included city governments, school districts, a rural Arts and Humanities Council, and other community groups. For the last six years he has lived in New York City, where he is the executive director of New Dramatists.

He is the author of *The Playwrights' Handbook* and *Scenes and Monologues from the New American Theatre* (coauthored with Frank Pike). Later this year his book *Interviews with Pulitzer Prize–Winning Playwrights* will be published by Prentice Hall. He also has written thirty produced plays and numerous newspaper and magazine articles on a wide variety of topics.

The Playwrights' Handbook (with Frank Pike)

Scenes and Monologues from the New American Theatre (with Frank Pike)

Interviews with Pulitzer Prize–Winning Playwrights

How to Shake the New Money Tree

5-6-88

How to Shake the New MONEY TREE

Creative Fund-raising for Today's Nonprofit Organizations

THOMAS G. DUNN

ROUND LAKE
AREA LIBRARY

PENGUIN

PENGUIN BOOKS

Published by the Penguin Group
Viking Penguin Inc., 40 West 23rd Street,
New York, New York 10010, U.S.A.
Penguin Books Ltd, 27 Wrights Lane,
London W8 5TZ, England
Penguin Books Australia Ltd, Ringwood,
Victoria, Australia
Penguin Books Canada Ltd, 2801 John Street,
Markham, Ontario, Canada L3R 1B4
Penguin Books (N.Z.) Ltd, 182–190 Wairau Road,
Auckland 10, New Zealand

Penguin Books Ltd, Registered Offices:
Harmondsworth, Middlesex, England

First published in Penguin Books 1988
Published simultaneously in Canada

Copyright © Thomas G. Dunn, 1988
Foreword copyright © David Durenberger, 1988
All rights reserved

Page 185 constitutes an extension of this copyright page.

LIBRARY OF CONGRESS CATALOGING IN PUBLICATION DATA
Dunn, Thomas G.
How to shake the new money tree.
1. Fund raising. 2. Corporations, Nonprofit.
I. Title.
HG177.D86 1988 658.1'5224 87-8795
ISBN 0-14-046811-0

Printed in the United States of America by
R. R. Donnelley & Sons Company, Harrisonburg, Virginia

Set in Aster
Designed by Victoria Hartman

Except in the United States of America, this book is sold subject to the condition that it shall not, by way of trade or otherwise, be lent, resold, hired out, or otherwise circulated without the publisher's prior consent in any form of binding or cover other than that in which it is published and without a similar condition including this condition being imposed on the subsequent purchaser.

Foreword

How to Shake the New Money Tree provides an easy "how-to" guide to a new, alternative approach to fund-raising for nonprofit organizations of every size and variety and in every type of community. The nonprofit industry, encompassing 857,512* organizations nationwide, is the third-largest industry in America, and fund-raising is the lifeblood of its existence. Throughout the late sixties and early seventies, donors (corporations, foundations, and individuals) were reaping the benefits provided by government incentives for supporting nonprofits. In the late seventies, this era of government-encouraged fund-raising ended. The earlier "What do *you* need?" approach to giving was replaced by an "What can *I* get for my money?" attitude by potential donors. As the budget cuts continue and tax laws become even more restrictive, the typical fund-raising methods of the past fifteen years are fast becoming obsolete. This book describes alternative methods of fund-raising—be it a theater party, street fair, commercial tie-in, auction, direct-mail campaign, program advertising, fashion show, baseball game, sponsorship, membership, or two dozen other "Show Me" techniques in which the donor gets the "something" tangible for his money.

It guides the reader, step-by-step, into choosing and im-

*As of 1985, per Independent Sector.

plementing the "Show Me" techniques developed in recent years across the country. Arts organizations, church groups, hospitals, scout troops, charities, and every other type of nonprofit group will find dozens of innovative but proven survival tactics to ensure their continued operation and growth in today's challenging financial climate.

Unlike more traditional fund-raising methods that require organizations to meet eligibility guidelines set by funding sources, the "Show Me" approach allows each organization to be in complete control of its own fund-raising efforts. Using the techniques in this book, even a lone individual with nothing but a dream (no money, no staff, no supporters) can generate enough money to create and fund a new organization. And as the reader will learn, the variety of "Show Me" fund-raising methods are as limitless as the organization's collective imagination.

The author of *How to Shake the New Money Tree* has been working in the fund-raising field for two decades. Thomas G. Dunn started his own nonprofit theater in Minneapolis in the late sixties and since that time has run nonprofit theaters in Ohio and New York. He has personally raised over $3.5 million dollars with less than $250,000 of that coming from the government. Besides his direct work with nonprofit arts groups, he has also worked as a fund-raising consultant to some forty different organizations, including a twenty-one-county rural consortium of local humanities councils, a suburban park and recreation department, several school districts, nursing homes, and civic organizations. Currently, he is the executive director of New Dramatists, a national theater service organization.

Tom Dunn represents all sides of the fund-raising business. He is the professional, raising $500,000 a year, who started his career working with community groups and amateur companies with budgets of less than $50,000. Mr. Dunn has learned through experience how to give contributors something for their dollar so that they will become and remain avid supporters of the organization soliciting their aid.

How to Shake the New Money Tree gives the reader a historical perspective on the field of nonprofit fund-raising, shows how and why it is the way it is today, and guides him through the many ways for his organization to grab a good piece of the pie. *How to Shake the New Money Tree* gets the reader thinking differently—thinking in terms of alternative "Show Me" fund-raising techniques that will safeguard the survival and good health of his organization throughout the rest of the twentieth century and beyond.

—SENATOR DAVID DURENBERGER

Acknowledgments

I'd like to thank all of the people who taught me about both the art and the craft of fund-raising over the years: Ted Crawford, Cynthia Gehrig, Robert Crawford, Ruth Humleker, Robert Kingsley, Arthur Ballet, Hugh Southern, Al Heckman, Orel Thompson, Pam Michaelis, George White, Amy Lynn, and many others.

Thanks especially to Laurie Sammeth, whose typing and editing skills and fund-raising know-how got this book ready.

Contents

Foreword by Senator David Durenberger vii
Acknowledgments xi
Introduction xv

1 : SOME HISTORY 1

2 : THE "SHOW ME" APPROACH 12

3 : GOALS AND METHODS 20
Setting Goals 21
Selecting Methods 23
A One-time Project 30
An Ongoing Program 33
Sample "Show Me" Techniques 37
Special Membership Drives 52
Advertising Space Sales 58

4 : PLANNING 64
Volunteers 64
A Timeline: Press Releases, Direct-mail Campaigns, Door-to-door Drives, "Free" Concerts 72
Corporate Sponsorships 92

5 : SPECIAL EVENTS 107
Nuts-and-bolts Planning 107
Media Coverage 115
Eleventh-hour Tricks 118

6 : TROUBLESHOOTING 122
Special Events 123
Organizations 134
Direct Mail 139
Corporations and Foundations 143

7 : FOLLOW-UP 148
Fourteen "Do's and Don'ts" 148
A Last Word 159

Appendix A: Glossary 165
Appendix B: Foundations 179

Introduction

I want to get rich, get famous, and get laid.
—Bob Geldof in an interview, 1981

We can build wells and give them a life. I prefer to do that.
—Bob Geldof in an interview, 1985

In just four years Bob Geldof seems to have undergone a radical transformation. His beliefs, his goals, and his very relationship with the world have been altered so completely that it's hard to believe they originated in the same brain.

Who is Bob Geldof? According to *Time* magazine in January 1986, he is "the elf with the spiritual mission." *Time* further elaborated:

> The real Bob Geldof is, in fact, a full-hearted rock musician with a stalled career and a tempestuous conscience who launched, almost casually, a musical mobilization to aid starving people in Africa. What he pulled off, and what he inspired, still seems something like a fantasy. A single record by a group of British rock stars organized by Geldof under the rubric "Band Aid" raised $11 million. The Live Aid Concert, held in London and Philadelphia the same July day and broadcast live around the world, brought an additional $72 million. . . .

Time was but one of the publications that touted Bob Geldof as a Nobel Peace Prize candidate in 1985, and he was knighted for his efforts by Queen Elizabeth II in 1986.

What happened? What caused this deep-seated personality change to occur? We can only speculate about the details, but one thing is obvious. Bob Geldof was so touched, so upset over the plight of the starving Africans, that he reversed his priorities. The nature of his challenges became not personal but public. These public concerns motivated Bob Geldof to seek and develop ways to motivate others to support these concerns.

The federal government may have indirectly had a part in this reversal—if not for Bob Geldof, then for millions of Americans. Looking on the positive side, as the government's concerns move farther and farther away from the arts and social sciences and more and more requests for funding are turned down, the consciousness of the nation is being raised. The practice of fund-raising has moved from the dark realm of things that "decent people don't do" or the remote domain of government and "old money" to something actively pursued by everyone from movie stars to clergymen to corporate leaders.

Bob Geldof could be called one of the high priests of the new fund-raising philosophy. His works could be described as the ultimate "Show Me" approach to solving problems with creative donor-oriented fund-raising techniques. Bob Geldof turns consumers into supporters of nonprofit organizations by offering them something—a record, a rock concert, an athletic event—that they already want and would buy for themselves anyway. He appeals to people's self-interests in the service of a higher cause.

In just a few years since Geldof started the "Show Me" fund-raising bandwagon rolling with Band Aid and Live Aid, these large-scale fund-raising extravaganzas have become a familiar part of all of our lives. Whether we've actually participated in any of these fund-raising efforts or not, none of us has escaped the widespread publicity they attract. Glittering with celebrities, Live Aid and its successors and imitators—Farm Aid I and II, Sport Aid, Hands Across America—have proven to be very effective fund-raising techniques, uncovering nonprofit supporters from a whole new segment of our population. Even the Soviet Union has recognized the effectiveness of the "Show Me" methodology. Russia's top pop and rock music stars performed in a Moscow concert held to raise money for the Chernobyl nuclear disaster fund just a month after the disaster itself.

Bob Geldof has another important lesson to teach. As we tackle the new fund-raising in the last gasp of the twentieth century, we must not lose sight of our real goals. We must not focus on raising funds without simultaneously keeping in mind the purpose for which these funds are being raised.

Geldof's 1986 effort in support of African famine relief, Sport Aid, built around an international "Race Against Time," generated funds through ticket and T-shirt sales and corporate sponsorships. But in a January 8, 1986, *Newsweek* article, Geldof stressed that money was the secondary motive. "This is primarily a demonstration of feeling. It puts intolerable pressure on those sitting in the U.N. the next day to reappraise how they look at the continent."

We all must keep our fund-raising efforts in their proper perspective. As the cartoon on the next page, from the *San Francisco Chronicle,* illustrates, Hands Across America (or any other nonprofit fund-raiser) is not meeting its goal if all it raises is money. We must continually fight to raise people's consciousness so that they will take on the concerns of our particular cause or program as their own. If people only pay their $10, hold hands for fifteen minutes, and thereby feel that they have done their part about hunger (or whatever the problem) and can now go back to their daily lives without a second thought, we are in danger. We must be careful to use the new fund-raising not only to raise funds but also to serve as a jumping off point to garner real awareness and ongoing support of every kind for our concerns.

Now it's time for us—no matter what our idea or activity, no matter how large or small our organization—to learn how we too can meet our particular challenges with creative "Show Me" fund-raising approaches.

But before we leave Bob Geldof and his remarkable efforts, he has asked that as many publications as possible that write about his work include the address to which contributions can be sent:

> The Live Aid Foundation
> P.O. Box 7800
> San Francisco, California 94120

HOW TO SHAKE THE NEW MONEY TREE

chapter 1

SOME HISTORY

Grantland is the creation of Grant Brownrigg, who recently returned to the business world after spending nine years at the helm of three major arts organizations. The strip, which appears regularly in *Center Arts*, takes a good-natured poke or two at advocacy, fund-raising, committees, budgeting, and boards of directors.

Fund-raising is as old as recorded history. The search for the Golden Fleece was a one-time-only project that had donors lining up to be part of this unique adventure. The Wooden Horse of *Iliad* fame was a capital improvement that helped the larger society to achieve a history-making goal. It was the ongoing support and contributions of not only the Greek city-state governments but also the individuals and developing merchant and agricultural companies that allowed the Golden Age of Drama to become a reality in fifth-century Greece. Enlightened—and surely, not-so-enlightened—human beings, either individually or in corporate units, made life in ancient Greece the cultural paradise it was. These people understood not only how to *give* money but also how to *get* money. Whether it be Marco Polo's travels or the building of Notre-Dame, the high points of mankind's history have been made possible through fund-raising efforts.

In our own time the first great shift in fund-raising occurred in 1913 with the passage of the income tax laws. Until then the same type of appeal for funds had been made for years and years: "Please give us support. If you do so, the community will benefit." This is known as the direct appeal. It isn't subtle. It relies solely on one's altruistic qualities, but is not an unworthy approach by any means and will work with some people in some situations. What the passage of the income tax laws did for fund-raising, however, was to give people an additional incentive to donate money. A few years after the onset of the income tax came the concept of the tax "write-off," or deduction. The government added these deductions for charitable contributions to the tax laws as a way to promote fund-raising efforts for the good of the populace. The write-off from such donations eventually became more popular than, say, the annual symphony season they were supporting.

Before World War II only the very, very wealthy used such deductions for two reasons: The income tax laws were so new that only the rich had the kind of financial advice needed to understand the use of tax deductions, and, outside of churches and schools, very few bona fide nonprofit organizations existed at this time. While most major cities had a museum or two and a symphony existed here and there, there were no social service organizations, no experimental theater companies, and no self-help or hobby clubs operating under nonprofit banners. The major supporters of the relatively few existing nonprofit organizations were the trustees of these organizations—philanthropists of the old school with a new twist: Not only could they feel good about contributing to the benefit of mankind in some way, but now they could save themselves a few pennies (or hundreds or thousands of dollars) in the bargain.

Since World War II the situation has changed dramatically and rapidly. From less than 1,000 nonprofit organizations in the country in 1946 (excluding churches and schools), there were easily some 200,000 by 1980. (Including churches and schools, this number jumped to 857,512 by 1985). What happened? By 1985 some $79.8 billion was being given by the private sector to support nonprofit activities. Did the IRS loosen up that much in allowing tax write-offs for contributions to charities?

No. If anything, the IRS became more strict. Instead, the American people—all of them, rich and poor but mostly middle-class—started giving more because the nonprofit fund-raisers learned how to ask for it. Fund-raising as an art and a science came into being and produced amazing results.

A second great shift occurred in 1969 with the passage of the Tax Reform Act, which fundamentally altered the makeup of foundations—tax-exempt organizations created to distribute money that has been earned as interest on an endowment to nonprofit organizations. Prior to 1969 the IRS required very little reporting from foundations, who therefore operated very much out of the public eye. For the most part, "fund-raisers" were actually members of the upper class whose fund-raising efforts were acomplished far more often than not over dinners with friends rather than over a typewriter in an office. It was a quiet profession with major gifts only occasionally announced in newspaper society columns of "Arts and Leisure" sections. Hospitals, symphony orchestras, national youth organizations, and the like were started and sustained by a relatively small percentage of the population for the good of the whole.

After 1969, however, foundations had to report regularly to the IRS on where they donated their funds, and these reports, the 990 Tax Return, became available to the public. For the first time, it was possible to find out not only how much money the Mellon Foundation, say, donated in a given year but also to whom they gave it. A variety of organized and timely reference publications with all kinds of pertinent information on grant-making organizations and their grantees became easily accessible through the public library. Guidebooks and seminars on how to ask for money popped up in communities across the nation, and some colleges offered degree programs in fund-raising. Secrecy turned to knowledge. Elitism opened up to democratic competition. Fund-raising as a science and a profession was born.

Another significant change made by the 1969 Tax Reform Act was the requirement that foundations now give away all of what they earned each year on their assets as well as a small percentage of those assets themselves so they ultimately operate to go out of business. This reform halted the use of foundations as investment vehicles that could generate great sums of tax free wealth, but it also meant that the bulk of the burden for supplying nonprofit funds has shifted over to corporations and individuals. According to *Giving U.S.A., 1985,* the annual study by the American Association of Fund-Raising Counsel, of the $79.8 billion given to nonprofit organizations by nongovernmental sources in 1985, only $4.36 billion came from foundations—or less than 6 percent of all private giving. However, foundations continue to play a vital role in the fund-raising world, both because they tend to give much larger gifts than do corporations, and because they are seen as the leaders in picking the best and most promising organizations to fund, so I discuss them further in Appendix B, pages 178–83.

Corporate giving has increased tremendously since the sixties. According to an advertising supplement entitled "Corporate America" in the May 1986 issue of *Natural History* magazine, "some corporations in recent years have almost alone equaled the total level of corporate cultural support in the late 1960s." The Business Committee for the Arts (BCA), a group of corporate executives organized in 1967, reports that in 1969 a few dozen companies gave $22 million to the arts. By 1982 many more corporations had joined the effort and gave over $500 million. BCA's goal for its twentieth anniversary is to go over the billion-dollar mark in business support of the arts.

The willingness of corporations in this country to serve and often support people, ideas, and organizations such as yours is exemplified by the Mellon Bank's offering of a free book with tips on how to get a grant. Titled *Discover Total Resources: A Guide for Nonprofits,* it is available by writing to Mellon Bank, 1 Mellon Center, Pittsburgh, Pennsylvnia 15258. I will discuss further methods of getting corporate support in Chapter 4.

When the Great Society programs of the sixties began to reach their maturity, government became involved in a major way in everything from job training (such as the mammoth Comprehensive Employment and Training Act or CETA program) to highway beautification projects to all kinds of support for the poor and disadvantaged. Professional fund-raisers could start a major drive knowing they had a good chance of getting the federal, state, and city governments (and in many areas also the county government) to meet a major portion of the needs of this drive. Corporations and foundations often made up the rest.

If individuals were called on at all, they usually were selected from the ranks of the traditional funders and supporters of major nonprofit organizations. Some organizations, such as the National Geographic Society and the American Red Cross, did supplement their lists of supporters for major drives with a "membership" drawn from the general public. However, the pressure to develop a "broad base of support" with as many individual contributors as possible—so important today—was still relatively insignificant in the late sixties and early seventies.

By the mid-seventies, however, the words "broad base of support" turned into a catch phrase among fund-raisers nationwide. As we emerged from the discontent of the sixties and the political upheavals caused by Vietnam and Watergate, we found ourselves both socially conscious and seemingly desirous of being united as a nation once more. By the time of Jimmy Carter's inauguration, funding sources, reflecting the moods and interests of the country at large, were adamant about supporting programs that could demonstrate this "broad base of support." In the case of the arts, for instance, major foundations and corporations were rearranging their priorities and felt that programs they had supported heavily for years should now begin to be supported more by these other "broader bases of support."

By the time of Ronald Reagan's first inauguration, there were new catch phrases that included words like "ongoing importance," "fiscal responsibility," "predictable growth," "track record," "evidence of independence," and "future funding." The message being delivered in one form or another by this new phraseology is that new ideas are not going to have such an easy time of it. The government—and thus, the money—is moving away from the social programs. If you are starting a community orchestra, chances are good that it will be quite a few years before you'll be able to secure any government funding for your efforts. What money the government does allot to your field will be divided among the major orchestras that have long, established histories.

Thus, a major thrust of fund-raising efforts has been toward individual contributors (often called "members"). According to *Giving U.S.A.*, in 1985, 82.7 percent of all charitable contributions ($66 billion out of a record total $79.8 billion) came from individual contributors. Far outdistanced in second place the same year were corporations and foundations, who each gave about $4.3 billion. For the first time in sixteen years, individual Americans gave more than 2 percent of their personal income to philanthropy. In one year individual giving increased by almost $6 billion.

Factors leading to this significant jump include the maturing of the "baby boomers." In an article by Kathleen Teltsch in *The New York Times* on May 12, 1986, Dr. Ralph L. Nelson, a Queens College economist, states, "We can look forward to more Americans in the prime giving years" as the numbers of people in the 35–65 age goup increase. Corporate giving, on the other hand, was expected to show "only moderate growth for the remainder of the eighties." The federal government has mandated that we look to private sources for support of nonprofit activity in this country. In fact, there have been two serious efforts to limit or abolish deductions for nonprofit contributions in the last few years, but each effort has been defeated in Congress. The largest means of nonprofit support by far is the individual contributor. According to *Time* on June 16, 1986, "Nearly nine out of ten Americans report making some contribution to charity."

Despite all the statistics, however, the individual remains the least understood and the least tapped source of support of nonprofit activities.

The Fund-Raising Institute's William F. Balthaser cautions that overlooking the individual can lead to doom:

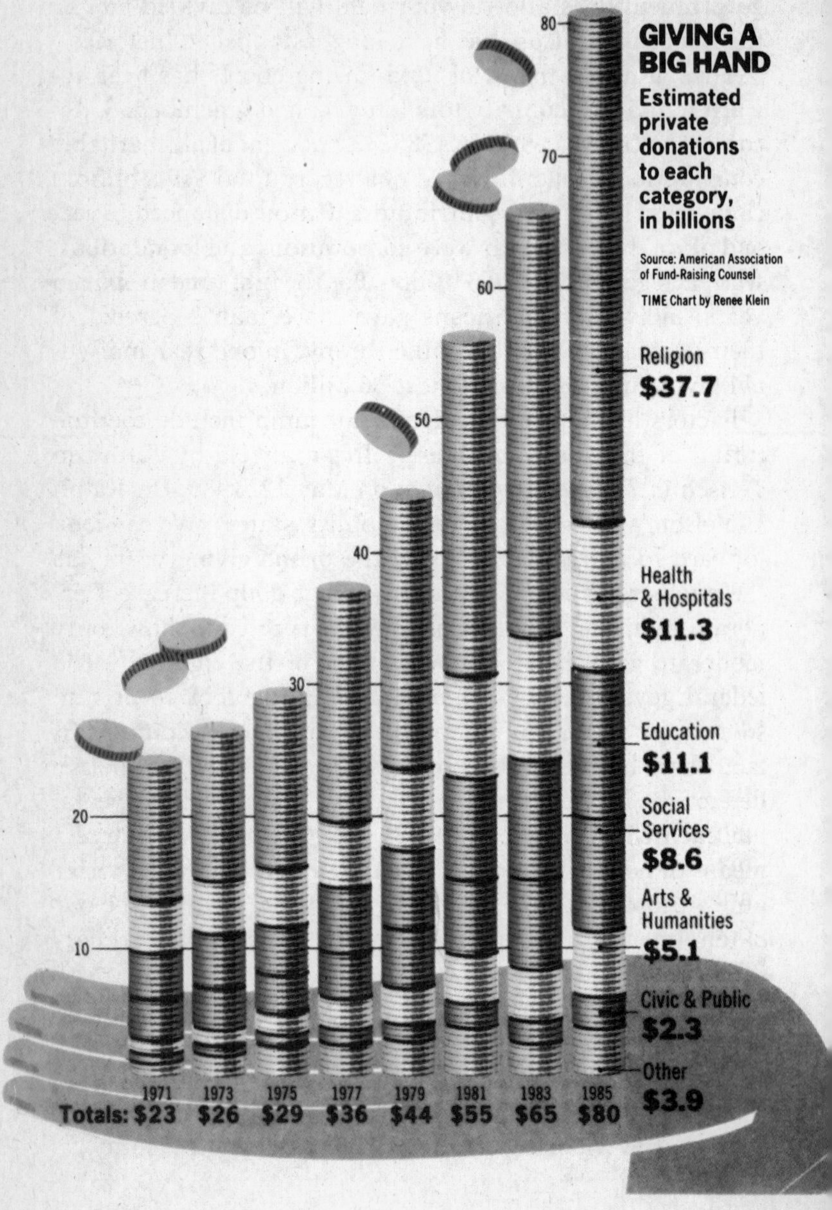
GIVING A BIG HAND
Estimated private donations to each category, in billions
Source: American Association of Fund-Raising Counsel
TIME Chart by Renee Klein
80
70
60
50
40
30
20
10
Religion $37.7
Health & Hospitals $11.3
Education $11.1
Social Services $8.6
Arts & Humanities $5.1
Civic & Public $2.3
Other $3.9
1971 1973 1975 1977 1979 1981 1983 1985
Totals: $23 $26 $29 $36 $44 $55 $65 $80

> The leading failure factor turned out to be simple and obvious: The programs that lost the most money had *never solicited their prospects!* Why? The people in charge avoided personal solicitation like the plague, didn't know how to do it, didn't know how to train others, were scared of it. But the individual prospect is where the big money is for most charitable causes—80 to 90% of the total gift potential.

As we turn our focus away from government and private and corporate foundations, we put aside the old methods of formal applications and proposals. At the same time, we must develop new methods to win the support of our new audience: the individual contributor. We must try to discover what motivates, what reaches, what most forcefully convinces people to turn over some of their money in support of our particular projects and programs.

Most nonprofit groups that survived the fluctuating funding patterns of the seventies ended up with sizable mailing lists of contributors. Once upon a time it was thought that once having established this "broad base of support," the continued existence of a nonprofit organization would be ensured, even during periods when public support declined.

In the eighties too many groups have discovered too late that this theory does not hold true. With the cutback in government funds and the proliferation of nonprofit organizations, there is now intense competition for what funds are available. A person accustomed to making an annual donation to the same museum or choral group year after year is now receiving appeals from several museums and several choral groups.

So who gets the money? The group that does the most exciting work, that draws the most publicity to itself, and, especially, the group that puts forth the most tantalizing appeal for funds.

To appreciate the significance of the individual appeal,

let's look ahead. Whether the Republicans or the Democrats win the next presidential election will not have much of an effect on governmental policies of funding for some time. The cutbacks in government support made during the Reagan adminstration are not funds that can be restored immediately. Congress is a cumbersome arbiter of funding "trends."

Private foundations and corporations have been plugging holes in the dike for too long to be able to bounce back and set new funding trends when a new Administration comes into power. The challenge of filling the funding gap left by the Reagan administration will remain with corporations, foundations, and especially individuals into the year 2000 and beyond. We members of the general public have become much more aware of the important roles we play funding important programs.

The new "awareness" or "social consciousness" by the general public will not ensure the success of your organization's funding campaign, however. Beginning with the introduction of the income tax deduction in 1913, people—and corporations and foundations—are used to getting something tangible in return when they give.

The crux—and the challenge—of today's creative fund-raising is finding tangible rewards that will stand out in a very crowded field.

Resource List: Chapter 1

If you are starting to get interested in the field of fund-raising, here are a few general resources that you might consider looking into:

Grassroots Fund-raising Journal
P.O. Box 14754
San Francisco, California 94114

Nonprofit World Report
published bimonthly by
The Society for Nonprofit Organizations
6314 Odana Road, Suite 1
Madison, Wisconsin 53719

Foundation Directory
published by
The Foundation Center
79 Fifth Avenue, Eighth Floor
New York, New York 10003

The Successful Volunteer Organization
by Joan Flanagan
published by Contemporary Books, Inc.
180 North Michigan Avenue
Chicago, Illinois 60601

Independent Sector
Various publications are available from
1828 L Street, N.W.
Washington, D.C. 20036

chapter 2

THE "SHOW ME" APPROACH

Imagine charging $500 in airline tickets on your Visa card, knowing that $2.50 will automatically go to fight environmental pollution, support feminist causes or aid the homeless—at no additional cost to you. Such a credit card would bear the logo of your favorite charitable or politically active organization, and beneath the inscription might be a four-color image of mountains and streams or an impressionistic likeness of a woman's face.

—From an article in *The New York Times,*
February 7, 1987

What exactly is the "Show Me" approach to fund-raising? The term itself was coined by Laurie Sammeth, who worked with me on this book and who has several years of fund-raising experience both in New York City as general manager of New Dramatists and in Tucson, Arizona, as a board member of Orts Theatre of Dance. In our work together we've come to recognize the importance of giving people something for their dollar, and that very simply is what we mean by the "Show Me" approach.

This broad definition encompasses a huge diversity of activities. Amy Lynn, a veteran New York City nonprofit board member and special event coordinator, practices "Show Me" methodology by selling duplicate manuscripts and books from a performing arts library at a Sunday afternoon fair or by producing a Broadway-type revue for a Lincoln Center benefit. We at New Dramatists have given away silk scarves and designer perfumes (all donated free of charge by companies looking for promotional credit) at our annual fund-raising luncheons.

The "Show Me" approach can be very effectively used with corporate sponsorships as well. Some major fast-food retailers have held promotions in which a certain percentage of their sales goes to benefit a nonprofit organization. Last year in St. Louis, for instance, for every Big Mac McDonald's sold over a one-month period, 10¢ went into the coffers of that city's United Arts Fund.

"Show Me" techniques range from the conservative to the most radical. On a more traditional note, the National Gallery of Art in Washington, D.C., is carving the names of all $10,000-plus donors onto the walls of the museum, while the names of smaller donors are being inscribed in a permanent book that is on display.

A more daring use of the "Show Me" theory was used by the New York University School of Law. The card reprinted on the following page was sent to 8,500 alumni of the school in an envelope with a depiction of an outsized hand about to grab some dollar bills. These blunt tactics worked quite well to bring in funds but did receive some criticism. Charles R. Feldstein, president of a thirty-two-year-old Chicago fund-raising counseling firm, attacked it in a December 1985 *New York Times* article: "We should stay within the ken of good taste. . . . The IRS only does what Congress orders it to do and if we don't like what happens, we should change the tax law."

Norman Redlich, Dean of the Law School, replied in NYU's defense, "I put pressure on people to do things with style, class and a little different, just as I like NYU to be an organization with style, class, and a little different." NYU has focused their fund-raising efforts on the "broad base of support" concept in each of its schools since 1975 and has been a leader in the field of college fund-raising ever since.

Whether or not this new "Show Me" approach appeals to everyone's sense of good taste or ethics, there's no question that it works. As David Rockefeller noted at a meeting of the Independent Sector, a coalition of 640 leading foundations, corporate donors, and national nonprofit organizations, "The recent rock concerts and record sales for African famine relief have opened up a whole new vista of philanthropy which would have been inconceivable only a few years ago." Rockefeller gave a further nod to "Show Me" philanthropy in a June 16, 1986, special issue of *Time* magazine when he posed the question, "If Tina Turner and Mick Jagger can have fun while raising money, why can't the rest of us?"

With the successes of new types of fund-raising ventures, it is easy to get caught up in a mood of euphoria. Lest the "Show Me" approach seem like a panacea handed down by the gods to solve all our funding problems, I want to mention some of the particular pitfalls and challenges that come with it.

First, because the "Show Me" approach works, more and more organizations are incorporating it into their fund-raising plans. Competition arises not just over which group has the most intrinsic value, but which one makes the most appealing offer to the contributor. If a community's public service radio station offers a tote bag for every donation during its membership campaign, while the local public service television station offers a trip to Bermuda, guess who's going to get more money?

This competition for the best "Show Me" offering is a challenge to every organization, but especially to those who don't have a great deal of money. A contemporary dance company in Arizona was just starting out and had no extra funds to spend on incentive items, so they first planned to offer a button with their logo for each purchase of a season subscription. (Unfortunately, you can't just give out a button anymore and expect to see good results. We are all buttoned, T-shirted, and bumper-stickered to death. When this was pointed out to them, they had to engage in some creative problem-solving. A new group with neither big bucks nor established corporate connections nor show biz contacts, they had to find something low-cost and appealing to their typical audience's interests. Without using any up-front monies, the company offered potential subscribers invitations to opening night cast parties and special subscriber-only events (at which members of the company would donate their time to hold discussions, demonstrations, and question-and-answer periods). With a small ticket discount and the promise of preferred seating at all concerts, the subscription campaign did very well.

* * *

Some of my favorite "Show Me" fund-raising techniques practices in recent years include:

Dartmouth College recently mailed stock certificates to 42,000 of its graduates. Ornately engraved on each certificate was the message: "You can save on taxes and invest in Dartmouth at the same time." In this case, the stock certificate serves a dual purpose, gathering cash contributions from alumni, and helping to get stock contributions. By pointing out the benefits of purchasing stock and donating it to the college (thereby avoiding capital gains taxes and simultaneously receiving a charitable gift tax deduction for the full amount of the stock purchase and all increases in its value), this appeal offers direct savings advantages to the contributor.

* * *

Lee Iacocca and Garrison Keillor are simply the best-selling among a growing number of authors who are donating all (in the case of Iacocca) or half (in the case of Keillor) or a percentage (in the case of most other authors) of their royalties to nonprofit causes. This doesn't mean you need to enlist the aid of a well-known author for your group, but it does suggest that any item or service people buy regularly could be a potential money-raiser.

In the last year alone the following programs have benefited from the generosity of authors. (And don't forget: As a result of this generosity, authors are able to avoid the double taxation that accompanies royalty payments.)

- Diabetes research (Iacocca).
- Minnesota Public Radio (Keillor).
- Statue of Liberty/Ellis Island Foundation (Leslie Allen's *Liberty, the Statue and the American Dream*).
- U.S.A. for Africa (Garry Trudeau).
- Drug abuse in Washington, D.C. (George Mendoza from *Norman Rockwell's Patriotic Times*).
- Lepers in Calcutta (Dominique Lapierre's *City of Joy*).

- AIDS research (Rock Hudson's portion of royalties from Sarah Davidson's biography of him, *Rock Hudson, His Story*).
- Vietnam veterans' jobs program (*Dear America,* a collection of letters from veterans, Bernard Adelman, Editor).

Not to be outdone, I'm donating half of the royalties of this book to the two nonprofit companies that gave me "on the job" training: The Playwrights' Center of Minneapolis and New Dramatists of New York City.

The Statue of Liberty restoration project got much of its money from selling commemorative items that sold from $1 to $5,000, including wood-carved clocks and gold and diamond lapel pin replicas of the statue with light-up torches from Tiffany's.

The Sierra Club has a VISA card deal with a bank so that every time a Sierra Club-VISA card is used, the Sierra Club gets a percentage of the profits from that transaction.

Kidspac, a political action committee that raises funds to promote child welfare concerns in Congress, cannot offer the traditional nonprofit tax deduction for contributions because it is a lobbying group. But Kidspac did enlist the aid of a philanthropist who supplies actual five-dollar bills that are mailed to potential large contributors, ostensibly to pay them for the time it takes to read the letters of appeal.

* * *

If these ideas seem too esoteric or expensive for you to consider, think back to your own youth. The seeds for the "Show Me" approach to fund-raising were no doubt sown when you cooked brownies for a school bake sale or washed cars for a church youth group fund-raiser. Every single person that contributed to your group got something for their generosity.

What is being described in this book is creative fund-raising. It is not the old-style fund-raising based on the camaraderie of the "old boy" networks. It is not the freewheeling, easy-come, easy-go fund-raising of the seventies based on massive infusions of federal support. This is fund-raising that will work in any type of financial climate—for anyone, anywhere.

Resource List: Chapter 2

The following are resources that the author turns to regularly for new ideas, inspiration and suggestions:

FRI Idea Pack

a compilation of ideas from monthly reports
Fund-Raising Institute
Box 365
Ambler, Pennsylvania 19002-9983

Dear Chris: Advice to a Volunteer Fund-raiser

by John D. Verdery
The Taft Group
5130 MacArthur Boulevard
Washington, D.C. 20016

Giving U.S.A.

by American Association of Fund-Raising Council, Inc.
25 West 43 Street
New York, New York

Where the Money Is: A Fund-raiser's Guide to the Rich

by Helen Bergan
BioGuide Press

P.O. Box 16072
Alexandria, Virginia 22302

Whole Nonprofit Catalog
by Grantsmanship Center
P.O. Box 15072
Los Angeles, California 90015

500 Ways for Small Charities to Raise Money
by Phillip T. Drotning
Public Service Materials Center
5130 MacArthur Boulevard
Washington, D.C. 20016

chapter 3

GOALS AND METHODS

Mr. Iacocca says that he simply won't go to luncheons anymore unless the organizers guarantee him a donation to his Statue of Liberty-Ellis Island Foundation of at least $1 million (plus, one presumes, complimentary meal with choice of beverage).

"I give a little speech, show a film, and then I put the hammer on 'em," he explains, puffing on a cigar in his Chrysler office in the Pan Am Building while telling how he and the private foundation he heads have raised more than $233 million to restore the statue and the crumbling buildings of Ellis Island.

"They can come in here, too," he continues, waving the cigar, "and have their picture taken with me for a hundred thousand."

—From *The New York Times Magazine,* May 18, 1986

Now there's someone who understands the power of "Show Me" fund-raising!

The *Times* further states that Iacocca's campaign "is credited . . . with having raised more money in a shorter period of time than any private fund-raising campaign before."

What? You say no one wants to pay $100,000 to have their picture taken with you?

Don't despair. What makes for Mr. Iacocca's success is no different from what can lead to your success in the fund-raising arena: a clear understanding of your goal, a commitment to it, and a method to reach it that offers your potential donors something they value.

Setting Goals

As with any project, the first step in launching a fund-raising campaign is setting a goal. To start, it helps to pinpoint the particular needs and resources of your organization—needs that will become goals and resources that will help you achieve them. Schedule time at a meeting of your board or staff or finance or development committee to work this out.

Mellon Bank's booklet *Discover Total Resources* strongly suggests conducting an annual self-examination to "determine who and what you are, where you want to be, and what you need to get there." Following is a reprint of their checklist for evaluating your organization:

State your purpose in two or three sentences.
List major accomplishments.
What community need do you serve?
Whom do you serve (include age, sex, race, income level, etc.)?
What services do you provide?
Who delivers your services (paid staff, volunteers)?
List strengths and weaknesses in each service area.
What other organizations (profit or nonprofit) provide the same services?
What is your performance rating compared to other providers?
Can you demonstrate public demand/support for your services?
What are your short- and long-term goals?
Are they consistent with your purpose and services?
Were your goals developed with input from:

Board?	Staff?
Consumers?	Volunteers?
Contributors	External consultants?
Members?	

Do you have an annual action plan, which includes:

Program objectives for each service?
Performance schedule?

Will your goals require a change in:

Number/type of persons served?	Financial support?
Services?	Volunteer support?
Staff?	Other?

What internal and external factor(s) could have a positive impact on your ability to achieve your goals?

What factors could have a negative impact?

What are your funding sources?

Memberships?	Businesses corporations?
Service fees?	Foundations?
Income-generating activities?	Government?
Individual donors?	Religious organizations?
Federated campaigns	Other?

What non-cash support do you receive?

Volunteers?	Services?
Goods?	Other?

After you've taken a good, honest, and thorough look at your organization (or your idea for an organization or project), concentrate on your immediate needs and identify specific goals:

1. Know your basic need.
2. Make a list of all the things you need to meet that basic need and set priorities, letting necessity dictate their order. You now have a list of your goals in the order you hope to accomplish them.
3. Rework each goal into clear, simple, step-by-step subgoals.

Now that you've set your project goals, you need to determine your financial goals. What will everything cost? Set down a range of low end and high end figures. It will give you more flexibility in your planning and greater ease in adjusting your budget, if necessary, as you go along.

Selecting Methods

There are many, many ways of achieving any fund-raising goal, some more effective in certain situations than others. Now that you've done the work to determine your needs and set your project and financial goals, you must devote equal attention to deciding how to reach these goals. Now comes the time to deal with what I think is the most interesting aspect of the "Show Me" approach to fund-raising: How do I select the "Show Me" method that will work best for my organization to reach this particular goal at this particular time with these particular donors?

What methods could you use? "Show Me" methodology knows no boundaries. The only guideline to go by when creating a "Show Me" technique is to make sure you are offering the potential donor something for his dollar, something he finds of value personally in some way. You must know your audience (your potential donors) well. Yet another barbecue may not have enough appeal in Schenectady but may seem very exotic and alluring to Manhattanites longing for a taste of the country.

The range of "Show Me" activities runs from the very simple through the elaborately detailed. The varieties of technique are literally as limitless as the resources of your organization's collective imagination. Later in the chapter, I will describe a couple of dozen successful "Show Me" techniques, but first let's examine how to go about selecting one.

There is no magic formula for choosing the fund-raising method that best suits your needs. Trial-and-error is the great teacher, but of little benefit as you start your fund-raising career. Much of the creativity in planning a fund-raising event or drive comes in deciding which method you'll use. As you read this book, as you read the newspapers, as you talk to your volunteers and gather ideas, there will be two or three ideas that strike you as interesting or crazy but—hopefully—promising. There you have the basis of your own fund-raising drive. Absolute success just cannot be guaranteed. You can't open this book or any book and find the perfect approach to raising money for your particular need. But we can work within a process that will go a long way toward tipping the odds in our favor. Let's work through this process, using a sample project as our model.

Step One: Conduct an internal examination of your organization's financial resources.

Let's say your goal is to help the youth of your community. You analyze the situation and decide that there is a need for youth to have some structured leisure-time activity available to them during the winter months. Your project goal is to build an ice skating rink. You need $5,500 to carry out this project, and hope to get contributions from a variety of sources. (It is always best to combine individual support with some contributions from local business or government. That way you never become too dependent upon any one source—an obvious disaster in the event that one pulls out. Also, individuals are more likely to give if the project has been endorsed by some larger, established source.) Analyze your available resources to come up with your financial goal for the project:

$5,500	=	total project cost
−2,000	=	contribution promised ($1,000 from city council; $1,000 from rink construction company)
$3,500	=	financial goal (to be raised from individuals)

Draw up a simple budget for this project that includes the cost of the project itself and also a figure for the expenses you will incur as you go about raising this money. How much should you allot for these fund-raising expenses? A rule of thumb is never to spend more than 20 percent of your financial goal for the project to raise the money. In the case of the ice skating rink, which has a project goal of $3,500, 20 percent for your expenses would be $700. It's wise to keep your expense budget as low as possible, so let's say you're going to budget $500 for fund-raising expenses.

Now there's a lot you can do with $500, and at the same time there is a lot you can't do with $500. You are not going to throw a black-tie dinner at a fancy hotel for $500, but you could do a mailing to a list of potential donors. You won't be able to produce a five-color brochure on the project for $500, but you could produce a very effective fund-raising letter with supporting documents. You won't be able to raffle off a new Cadillac for $500, but you might well throw a simple "Let's Build an Ice Skating Rink" day on the site of the proposed rink.

Step Two: Conduct an internal examination of your organization's social resources.

After all of the alternatives have been set out and you've narrowed down the list of fund-raising techniques in terms of your financial resources, look at your social resources as well.

- What types of contacts do our staff and board members have?
- What local celebrities can we call upon to add a touch of glamour?
- How many people can we mobilize to work on this project and what are their skills?
- What kind of media attention can we count on to publicize our efforts?

After adding up the financial and people resources available, you'll have a much clearer idea of what type of technique your organization can comfortably utilize to raise funds.

Step Three: Analyze and develop (i.e., cultivate) your audience. Now you must focus your attention on the audience for this technique, your potential donors. First, it's essential to identify your constituency—know who your current friends are and who your additional friends should be. It is time to make your shopping or prospect list.

Whom are you going to approach for funds in your drive? Who are the most likely candidates to lend support to the community by providing a place for its youth to skate? Developing a shopping list is your final step before actual fundraising begins.

Although I cannot overemphasize the importance of the shopping list, it is the most often ignored part of the fundraising process. Whether your goal is as simple as building an ice skating rink or as complex as setting up a nationwide school lunch program, *you must start with a shopping list.*

The first specific task to give to your volunteer committee (which we'll discuss further in the next chapter) is developing the shopping list. Everyone (including yourself) should participate by making a list of friends, family, and acquaintances who, either as individuals or in connection with businesses, may lend support to your project.

If six of you come up with ten names apiece, you'll have a good start on your shopping list, which will be your *primary list.* Make up a *prospect card* for each of these names that looks something like the following:

Sample Prospect Card

Name:____
Address:______________________________________
___________________________ Zip:__________
Phone: (day)____________ (eve.)______________
Any business/foundation affiliations:_____________
____
Recommended by:_________________________________

Once you have the primary list completed, develop a *secondary list*. Again, using your volunteers, discuss what people and businesses should be concerned about the youth in your community. This secondary list should be composed of people or small businesses who would logically share your interest in achieving your goal of building a new ice skating rink. It might include:

- Stores that sell sporting goods in your area.
- Local politicians. (Considering your goal, it would be difficult for any political leader not to lend support.)
- Any local sports celebrities or former sports stars.
- Prominent educators. (Superintendent of schools, school board members, and so on.)
- Doctors, dentists, lawyers, and other professionals who should be concerned about the youth of the community.
- Restaurants and other refreshment merchandisers in the area where the rink is to be constructed.
- Banks. (Usually concerned not only with the local community but with any and all construction within it.)
- Companies that would be approached to work on the rink construction. (See if any would consider giving you a "break" up-front in the fee that could be described as a leadership in-kind gift—see Appendix A, pages 165–77.)

The same type of prospect card (minus the "Recommended by" line) should be made up for each name on this secondary list. Make sure all the information (current address, phone, business title) on each card is correct. Be sure to update these cards if necessary when using them in the future.

If you come up with another forty names on this secondary list, added to those on your primary list, you suddenly have a good basis for a fund-raising drive of this size. With 100 prospects—more than half of whom you have direct contact with, which will be helpful later in follow-up—and a goal of $3,500, your individual goal for each prospect is now down to less than $40. In this day and age, that's the cost of a dinner out for two (or in New York City, for one). If you have drawn up a shopping list that is "solid" (composed of people with a real interest in your concerns and with this amount of money to spend), your goal should be very achievable.

Next, work out with your volunteer committee how best to use these primary and secondary donor lists to reach a final decision on the choice of "Show Me" method. Conduct a feasibility study by having your committee provide answers to questions like the following:

• How much can most of the people on the primary list afford? (Believe me, Mr. Iacocca knew exactly whom he was talking to when he put out his $1 million per lunch ultimatum.) If your committee members aren't sure that these friends and acquaintances can each come up with a $35 donation, you know you have a problem and need to adjust your plans accordingly. You may decide to alter your expense budget or get more names for your shopping list.

• What will they respond to best? A letter in the mail, followed by a phone call from someone they know? A visit as part of a door-to-door campaign? A party at the proposed site of the ice skating rink? Do they like to come to events outside their homes? Does it need to be something out of the ordinary?

• How much have they already given to the organization?

• Do they like to see their names on things (such as placques on theater seats and hospital ward doors)? In print?

If you decide to do some kind of special event, these questions should help you focus your choices:

• What types of events do they enjoy?

• What time of day is most convenient for them to attend? Day of week? Season?

• How much do they usually pay for entertainment?

Timing can be as crucial as the type of fund-raising plan you devise:

• What sort of timetable is best for this drive? Is it too close to Christmas? (Do most of these people have families that will require lots of extra gift expenses?) Is it too far away from Christmas? (If they don't have large families, would they respond well in a Christmas spirit?) Is it too near April 15 (tax time)? Can it be positioned as a last-minute tax deduction? Is it too near summer vacation time? Is it too near the drive that was held to build a new kiddie swimming pool to replace the one that was ruined in the big storm last summer? And finally, don't forget to look at the competition. Be sure to explore the other pulls on your prospects' purse strings:

• What projects have similar-sized organizations been successful with in the past?

• Has there been a proliferation of certain types of projects lately which would impede your success?

• What have other organizations planned for the same time period?

* * *

Now that you've completed an examination of your resources—financial and social—and know who your audience is, you will be able to choose the project with the most fund-raising potential for your organization.

A One-time Project

Let's walk through your final decision-making process. What techniques will you use to raise the $3,500 for the ice skating rink? We all—or at least those of us with a mailbox—are used to receiving appeals from Easter Seals, the local zoo, our church, our local politicians, and so on. Professional fund-raisers spend a great deal of money on sophisticated direct-mail campaigns using computer printout letters with computerized "handwritten" signatures by everyone from Katharine Hepburn to President Reagan. Generally, you can expect about a 2 percent return on a mailing of 100,000 or more. The fewer pieces you mail, the fewer the returns. Obviously, the huge computerized direct-mail campaign is not practical for most of you reading this book. On the other hand, given a small shopping list and a modest goal, direct mail is probably the simplest fund-raising approach. But how—with a shopping list of only 100 people—can you get a significant return? How do you increase your percentages?

FOLLOW-UP

Follow-up is one of the most important tenets of the "Show Me" fund-raising philosophy. The greatest mistake most volunteer groups make is to send out their letters of appeal and just wait for the checks to appear in the mailbox. You cannot expect any kind of a decent return without follow-up. The difference between 2 percent and 100 percent returns is planning and follow-up. With a thorough follow-up job, you can increase your percentages to close to a 100 percent return, something a big computerized mailing to tens of thousands will never get because there is no follow-up and the planning relies on a good mailing list and as general as possible a letter. The whole point of the "Show Me" approach is aim for 100 percent returns, and doing that requires extremely meticulous follow-up. It can mean the difference between success and failure. Follow-up phone calls, door-to-door visits, and personal notes are powerful "Show Me" tools that we will explore in detail later.

Now, back to our ice skating rink. Let's say your committee has conservatively decided that, on the average, all you can expect is $25 from each person on your shopping list. Even with a 100 percent return on your mailing to the 100 prospect names, that means you'll only raise $2,500—$1,000 short of your goal.

Don't worry. An individual fund drive should not be conducted solely through one fund-raising method. You will have a much better chance of reaching your goal by combining the mail drive with another "Show Me" technique. With some forethought, you can select complementary techniques, so that each not only brings in money on its own but stimulates increased giving through the other.

How will you raise the $1,000, plus expenses, to reach your goal? First, check on your finances. How much will the direct-mail campaign cost? How much of your fund-raising expense budget ($500) will be left to raise the additional $1,000? At 22¢ for postage, and approximately 40¢ for typing, stuffing, selling and stamping each letter (if done mostly by volunteers), and $60 for letterhead and return envelopes, your direct-mail campaign comes to $122, leaving $378 to spend on raising the rest of the money.

What would be the most effective way to spend this $378 to bring in those remaining dollars? This is where "Show Me" methodology really comes into play. Try to find a technique that's within your budget yet still offers that "something for their dollars" to contributors. How about holding a party on the rink site? A simple Saturday morning hot chocolate and doughnut affair would be inexpensive and would also generate publicity for your campaign.

Perhaps you could rig up a small skating rink in a portable swimming pool and recruit an amateur ice hockey player or figure skater to perform a demonstration of their skills. If the hot chocolate is donated (try your local grocery chain or fast-food restaurant—McDonald's, for example, recommends that each franchise keep on hand large portable soft drink dispensers for use at charity events as their public service to the community) and a certain number of doughnuts are given free for every dozen you buy, you can throw quite a party for $378.

How do you connect the party to the mail drive so that each will "feed" the other in building excitement and drawing in dollars? There are two choices. The rink party could be held to "kick off" the drive or it could be a way of wrapping up your mail campaign.

The "kickoff" party would have motivational benefits, a means of making people aware of the need for your drive. Following up the party with a timely mailing to its attendees may yield additional contributors. At the party itself you can pass the hat or suggest an admission fee/donation. An average of $5 per person from 300 people will give you the $1,500 needed to meet your goal and cover expenses.

Sounds pretty good. Frankly, this "kickoff" party scheme would be great for public relations, but a bit risky for fund-raising. Too many variables could work against your efforts: What if three hundred people don't show up or what if they don't want to give $5 each?

I recommend the second option—the "wrap-up" party at the end of the campaign after the mailing to your primary and secondary lists. Psychologically, people usually respond much better when asked to help finish off a fund-raising campaign rather than initiate it. If approached when the entire goal—in this case, $3,500—has yet to be raised, they may feel overwhelmed and less confident of the organization's ability to succeed, dissuading them from making a contribution. Also, at the start of a drive they may believe so many other people are being similarly approached that their input isn't so important; if they give at all, they tend to give in smaller amounts.

As the campaign nears its end, however, the sense of urgency builds. When a potential contributor hears that only a fraction of the entire goal is left to be raised by a certain deadline—say $965 of the original $3,500 by December 1—he sees the light at the end of the tunnel and gets caught up in the efforts to reach it. By holding your rink party at the end of the mail drive with a smaller portion of your final goal still outstanding, you are much more likely to get the attendance and donations that you need.

The guest list for the party could include community members living in the vicinity of the ice skating rink who will probably become its heaviest users. Invitations should also be made to everyone in your mail campaign, especially to those who haven't yet made a contribution. Thus, the wrap-up party serves as a follow-up to the mail drive and pulls in the stragglers, as well as prompting those who have already given to give more.

An Ongoing Program

Let's tackle a more complex fund-raising challenge. Once you've raised the money to build the ice skating rink—which the city has agreed to maintain—you're done. You've raised the $5,500 necessary to complete the project, and all of your contributors can see and use the results. It's a bit more difficult to raise money for a program that has ongoing expenses and offers things that do not appear in tangible form.

In 1980 I worked with a group concerned with the growing problem of teenage suicide. They decided to set up a twenty-four-hour telephone hot line for suicidal teenagers in their community. This project is unusual as fund-raising projects go; and it provides an important community service as well.

Let's say you and some other concerned citizens want to provide the same service for your community. Obviously, you want this service to continue as long as it is needed, which may, unfortunately, be for many years to come. How will your little band of responsible community members raise funds and oversee operations for such an ongoing program? You won't. The hot line is a good example of a program that, if it proves to be successful, can and should be taken over by an existing larger organization or agency. Once a need is shown and a solution discovered, it is often best to invite an established agency in the field to take over operation of the program.

Funding sources usually like this spin-off philosophy and feel much more confident about donating start-up money, if the fund-raising group plans to recruit ongoing future support from an agency or organization already at work providing similar services. If people (or corporations or foundations) know they won't continually be asked to fund a lasting program, they will be much more likely to contribute toward its start-up expenses.

Thus, your fund-raising task is to get support for a specified "start-up period" while giving your potential contributors a sense of confidence in the future of this program. One year is an appropriate time period to get the program under way and give it a track record with which to approach ongoing funding sources. In your fund-raising efforts for this first year, you do not need to (and most probably cannot) show potential donors that the future funding is in place, but you do need to show them that viable sources exist from which you can reasonably expect to get this ongoing support. The time to approach these long-term supporters is after the start-up monies have been raised and the hot line has been in successful operation for several months. (That's the "Show Me" the larger agencies are looking for.)

Now, to set the financial goal, target the audience and choose the "Show Me" methodology to raise the funds for the hot line's first year. Let's say a budget of $30,600 is your goal to start up and carry out the first year of the program. With a volunteer staff to run the hot line (many of whom may have helped with the fund-raising for the project), you are figuring $2,000 a month for operations expenses (including space rental, publicity, stationery, utilities, and so on), $1,500 for initial start-up expenses, and a onetime maximum allotment of $5,100 (20 percent of your projected financial goal—$25,500) for fund-raising expenses.

What fund-raising methodology will you use to raise this $30,600? Again, the best strategy is not to limit yourself to just one fund-raising method. Give yourself a two- or three-pronged "attack." That way, if one or even two of the methods don't meet their goals, you will have something to fall back on.

For the hot line I recommend using a three- to four-way method:

First, look for a governmental challenge grant to get the ball rolling. In the social service field federal government support is in a sharp decline, but many states and cities (and even counties and neighborhoods) have stepped in to fill the gap. A thorough researching of government agencies at various local levels should be your first step. The individuals who run these governing bodies do so to serve the needs of their citizens. Thus, a new solution to a growing problem, such as the hot line and teenage suicide, should be of interest to at least one government agency. If you can show you will be raising funds from two other sources (as we will outline below), the agency should be even more inclined to respond to your request.

How do you find those other two funding sources and

decide what methods to use to tap them? Go back to your original goal and the problem out of which it evolved. For the twenty-four-hour hot line you need fund-raising methods that will create the largest ground swell of community interest, concern, and even involvement. Involving as many individuals in your initial efforts as possible should lead to finding the volunteers to staff the hot line once it is set up. Door-to-door solicitation and a special event are two of the best ways I know to get that direct human contact that leads to involvement.

People in this country have a growing awareness of the alarming rate of teenage suicide. Facts and figures and ongoing publicity are at your disposal with the great number of magazine articles and books on the subject currently on the market. Since the public already knows about the problem, your job is to convince them your remedy is something *they* can help put into action. You want to stress to people that the ongoing operation of this hot line will improve the overall health and welfare of their community. Your door-to-door campaign, even if it doesn't generate a contribution from everyone, will create a personal contact that will be important in finding volunteers to run the operation. Use the twenty-four-hour hot line fund drive as a means to get to know the people it will be serving as well as a means to raise support money.

For the "Show Me" reward of the door-to-door campaign, let's hold a concert in honor of the hot line contributors at the close of the fund drive. This concert can complement the door-to-door campaign as well. Develop graduated levels of giving and "Show Me" returns to go along with each level: i.e., a $20 contribution gets you a free ticket to the concert; a $30 contribution, a free ticket and a bottle of perfume (which you get donated from the manufacturer or a local department store). In addition, you can set a cutoff date for contributions after which you will sell tickets (at a higher price) to people who did not contribute on the door-to-door campaign.

Chosen both for their individual merit and for the ways in which they complement each other, these three methods—the challenge grant, the door-to-door campaign, and the special event—should feed each other, causing each one to pull in far greater dollars than it would have if used alone.

An adjunct method of raising these hot line start-up monies would be to find corporate underwriting to cover your fund-raising expenses (the $5,100 that would go for the concert, printed materials, and so on). I will describe how to solicit these monies or in-kind contributions of goods and services in the next chapter on planning, but let me say now that trying to find corporate underwriting should be an integral part of almost any fund-raising campaign. Any money you don't have to spend raising money is money that can go directly into your project.

Sample "Show Me" Techniques

Now that we've seen how to select an appropriate "Show Me" methodology, here are a number of successful techniques that you may want to use or adapt or treat as inspirations to create your own activity.

The Private Party

A neighborhood bar in Seattle was having trouble drawing a crowd on Monday nights when the football season was over. A local community group dedicated to combating rape devised a scheme that was successful for each organization. On a Monday night they got a local band that needed exposure to play for free at the bar and created a private party atmosphere with decorations and homemade refreshments. A $10 cover charge included two drinks and the difference, plus the cost of any drinks over that, was split between the bar and the nonprofit organization. With very little effort, over $2,500 was raised, and some 150 new people got to know the bar, the organization, and the band. Holding private parties in public places, such as bars or restaurants or stores or art galleries, has a special appeal that works quite well to attract a large and profitable turnout.

The Movie Benefit

There are very few movie theaters that run twenty-four hours a day, seven days a week. Most of them can be approached to run a movie as a fund-raiser for a nonprofit organization, especially if the "cause" will serve to enhance that theater's standing in the community.

In San Jose, California, residents concerned about the problem of missing children in the community organized an old-fashioned "Sunday Afternoon at the Movies" for local families. Cartoons were rented inexpensively, and the movie theater donated the use of the building as well as the operating personnel. Proceeds from the ticket sales went directly to a fund to start a community day-care program and proceeds from concessions were split between the day-care fund and the movie theater. In between the short features, local law enforcement officials were given a chance to explain the problem and answer questions from parents and children on how to combat it. A total of $1,200 was raised; parents spent an enjoyable afternoon with their children; some community education took place in an interesting environment; and that movie theater was forever after thought of as a responsible member of the community.

Videocassette Promotions

A new variation on the movie theater benefit involves the videocassette. The National Fund for Runaway Children benefited when the Learning Corporation of America donated a portion of its revenue from the videocassette sale of *Streetwise*, a documentary about runaway children. A full-page ad announcing how this donation worked was put in national magazines by *Streetwise*'s distributor, New World Video, along with a plea for direct donations to the National Fund for Runaway Children that included its mailing address. Every organization participating in this promotion/fund-raiser served to support the goals of the other, leading to increased visibility and increased profits for all.

Progressive Dinner

Other crowd-pleasing "Show Me" events are those that involve that ever-popular American pastime: eating. Restaurants, especially those that have newly opened, quite often welcome ideas that will bring in new customers. Besides the standard dinners or luncheons, why not try a progressive dinner (where you move from place to place for each course) as the San Francisco Exploratorium Museum did for their fund-raiser? Five different restaurants participated, and each tried to outdo the other to see who could offer the best fare and the best service to back it up. The museum's supporters got to sample the fare at a variety of restaurants, and the outlay required by each establishment was thereby minimized.

Progressive Hotel Tour

The Seattle Repertory Theater came up with a variation on this progressive dinner idea. They held a progressive hotel tour with cocktail parties in the grandest hotel rooms in the city. People were fascinated to have the opportunity to view these rooms that they, as residents of the city, would never see otherwise, and the hotels were delighted to show off their accommodations.

Marathon Weekend

Taking advantage of a national craze, the Playwrights' Center of Minneapolis came up with a novel idea for a fund-raiser. They hosted a week-long Trivial Pursuit marathon. With very little effort and almost no expense, the event brought in over $6,000 and an amazing amount of publicity for the center.

Parade

Coney Island, U.S.A., now a thriving theatrical troupe with its own theater building, was only an idea in its director's mind when it raised almost $8,000 for start-up monies by holding a "beach opening" parade on the Brooklyn board-walk, funded by local merchants and individual residents who were delighted to participate in revitalization efforts of the area in which they lived and did business. That first parade, a mermaid parade, was so popular with Brooklyn-ites and the media that it's been an annual happening for five years now.

Celebrity Gala

To raise money for the New York Shakespeare Festival, *People* magazine hosted a tribute to Joseph Papp, Shake-speare Festival founder, in which they recreated Central Park (summer home of the festival) within a huge Manhattan ar-mory. According to *The New York Times,* "You could hardly see the decor for the people." Over two thousand individuals from the theater, magazine publishing, and advertising worlds attended. Many performed and others were enticed by the opportunity to mingle with the stars.

This benefit, of course, had the advantage of being able to draw on Public Theater alumni and the major advertisers and clients of *People* magazine. Before you rule out celebrity galas for your group, think. Who is "famous" (or infamous) in your community? Who could possibly draw people in? Be it the town mayor, local TV weather forecaster, radio disc jockey, restaurant owner, whoever, there are definitely people whose performance or speech or mere presence can form the basis of a "Show Me" event.

Picnic on a Barge

If Frank Sinatra doesn't live in your town, there are other means to draw people to your event. A Boy Scout troop in Troy, New York, raised the $450 necessary to cover the expenses of its annual retreat by making use of the unique resources its location had to offer. They held a "Picnic on a Barge," in which for $10 a head, attendees were served a hearty homemade meal (prepared and served by the Scouts) and listened to live music (played by troop members) as they floated down the river. The barge and soft drinks were donated free of charge. The first barge picnic was so well received that the Scouts have made it their annual fund-raiser.

"Insiders' Tours"

A Springfield, Illinois, elementary school made use of its proximity to the state capital in designing a fund-raising event to finance its extracurricular activities program. Enlisting the aid of an alumnus of the school who was now a state senator (and only too happy to receive this sort of publicity), they offered "Insiders' Tours" of the capitol building. The busloads of people on their way to the capital (driven by school bus drivers whose time was donated by the company) ended up receiving nightly news coverage as well, bringing in additional funds from sympathetic TV viewers.

Car Wash

If some of these ideas are beginning to seem a bit too grand for your needs, you can apply the same principles to a more grass-roots project. What could be a more pragmatic fund-raiser than a good old-fashioned car wash? Approach your local commercial car washing establishment for help. Offer to staff the place with your volunteers and split the profits. Again, for the sake of P.R. and the goodwill it affords them, a small businessperson can be readily convinced to underwrite a fund-raiser for your group.

NOTE: Bars, restaurants, miniature golf courses, movie theaters, and car washes are just a few fertile local business resources to explore when creating a "Show Me"-motivated fund-raising activity. Here, the "Show Me" principle works on an additional level. When a business organization cosponsors an event with you by providing its space and/or its services, it's profitable for you and good for business—present and future—for them. There are numerous ways to work out these mutually profitable collaborations.

Commercial Tie-ins

In Ottawa, Illinois (right down I-80 from Ronald Reagan's hometown), a June 1986 promotion by Handy-Mart stores followed the President's dictum that "Business should take up the slack." The chain had customers bring in their receipts at the end of the month and paid 1 percent of these totals to each person's favorite charity. Prompted both by practicality and altruism, both Handy-Mart and the charities benefited.

Likewise, in Cedar Rapids, Iowa, Camp Courage, a nonprofit summer camp for handicapped children, got Pepsi to donate 10¢ for every six-pack sold in the area to help send a child to camp.

Sports Events, Contests

There are many variations on the sports show fund-raiser. Baseball has always been very good about cooperating with nonprofits. Last year's "Great Airplane Toss," held in Minneapolis at the Minnesota Twins' Hubert H. Humphrey Metrodome, is an inspired example. Throughout the game volunteers sold sheets of paper at 50¢ each to more than 27,000 fans, who wrote their names and addresses on them and then folded them into airplanes. When the game was over, over 75,000 paper airplanes sailed through the air toward a new Mercedes-Benz parked in the field. Although no one succeeded in landing their plane inside the car, lesser prizes—from pizzas to vacations—were given out, and $35,000 in paper sales was donated to the National Kidney Foundation. Gate receipts were higher, and the sponsors got lots of publicity. The event was rescheduled for the following year.

A Day at the Ballpark

And don't forget that a wonderful fund-raiser is simply a day at the ballpark. Discounts on group tickets will be given, and local bus companies can be approached to provide free transportation. Free advertising can often be included as the team promotes your day at the park along with their regular ads and publicity, not to mention the possibility of making your pitch between innings. With the huge seating capacity of ballparks and the relatively minimal amount of arranging necessary on your part to pull it off, baseball (or football or basketball, etc.) fund-raisers are a tried and true "Show Me" favorite.

Miniature Golf Night

A high school band in Des Moines, Iowa, has made an annual event out of a fund-raiser at a miniature golf course in which the owner of the course donates *all* proceeds that are made on that night to the band. The band helps the owner staff the course for the night, does flyer posting, and gets publicity for the golf course (as well as for themselves, of course) on local radio stations and in the newspaper. On a nice night they claim that 300 people will play and that over $1,000 can be cleared when profits from homemade cookies and lemonade are added in. Again, both organizations together achieve far more than either could alone.

Celebrity Bowling

You'll find in your own community or in Hollywood or New York City that "celebrities" have the same complaint. They are always being asked to make appearances, ride in parades, speak at luncheons, and so on. So why not invite your local celebs to try something different in the way of helping out a good cause?

A new New York City theater company, Second Stage, asked twenty celebrities to join their supporters for a night of "celebrity bowling." Over 400 people paid upward of $100 a game to bowl with these luminaries. Minitournaments were held, and the celebrities even turned over their winnings to the theater. Over $20,000 was netted in the one evening. The bowling alley was delighted to get the publicity, the celebrities had a good time, and everyone went home happy.

Celebrity Boating

Enlisting the aid (and competitive spirit) of two young Kennedys, Ted Jr. and John F. Jr., the first John F. Kennedy Memorial Regatta was held to raise funds for the JFK Library in Dorchester, Massachusetts. Seventy-five boats paid a $25 entry fee each, which included a barbecue and clambake and a chance to win a prize.

A great example of "Show Me" technology, these contributors may have had little interest in supporting the library, but the library got their support by appealing to their personal interests.

Sports Stunts

There actually exist companies that specialize in providing donkeys who play basketball to help raise money at fund-raising events. If you prefer your athletes human, there are also companies that supply mud wrestlers. And these days there are more interesting substances in which to wrestle for money than mud. Promoter Bruce W. Rosenbaum specializes in arranging wrestling exhibitions in everything from chocolate pudding to creamed spinach for fairs and school fund-raisers.

Casino Nights

Physical activities may not be of interest to either your organizers or your potential givers, but one activity is a sure winner with everyone. Casino nights are easy ways to raise money for your organization while simultaneously ensuring that everyone attending—including the losers—takes something home.

There are a few key rules to follow when planning fund-raising events that involve gambling. Outside of that, you can be as free as good taste dictates in working out the rest of your house rules for the evening. The standard rules include:

1. Check with a lawyer and/or your local police about city and state statutes concerning gambling. (In all fund-raising events, you strive for an element of P.R., but a bust by the authorities is not a good way to get it.)
2. Be sure all winnings go to the "house" (your group).
3. Make sure everyone understands Rule 2 up-front. (There is nothing worse than winning at a night of Blackjack and suddenly getting the news that you must give it all back.) Make sure the rules of the night are clearly posted!
4. Have door prizes to give away, so winners (and losers) get something to take home with them.

Bake Sale

One of the simplest and oldest ways to raise money is the bake sale, but don't overlook the importance of planning because it seems such a simple idea. The reason some bake sales are more profitable than others is because of the way in which they are organized and run. Some hints:

1. Choose the site for the sale with care. Make sure it is well-traveled and as attractive as possible. (Local nonfood businesses will often let you use space in the front of their stores or showrooms since it increases their draw as well.)

2. If you're raising funds for a certain constituency, say senior citizens, have them bake the goods themselves. Milk the "homemade cookies by Grandma and Grandpa" or whatever for all it's worth—it'll promote sales and your cause at the same time, not to mention cutting your overhead way down.

3. Think of the project not only as a way to raise funds but also as a means to "spread the word." Prepare a simple flyer or letter stating your case and your needs and hand it out to every customer. Take advantage of the one-on-one human contact you have in this situation also. In a very low-key fashion, you might well be able to pull in extra donations above and beyond the baked goods sales.

4. Consider holding the bake sale on a regular basis, say once a week for a month to start. If you succeed in building a clientele for the goods, you have the start of an ongoing means of raising support monies and perhaps even the backbone of a nonprofit organization.

"Rent-a-Senior" Project

Projects that create a productive blend of constituents and cause are naturals when working with a group like senior citizens, many of whom have been unhappily forced into retirement. A great way to raise money *and* address this concern quite visibly is through the "Rent-a-Senior" project. Again, the overhead should be almost nil and the organization and operation quite smooth if preplanned carefully.

1. Develop a list of all the areas of expertise and interests among the members of your group. Include everything from

the seemingly insignificant to the most complex and incorporate these skills and interests into specific job titles.

2. Set a standard rate ($5 an hour as a contribution to your cause).

3. Set up a phone number and staff (with senior volunteers) where people can call in to hire.

4. Approach a local radio and/or newspaper to run an ad or article listing the jobs available, rates, and so on.

5. Send your seniors out with clear instructions as to where the job is and what the job is.

Soon your "Rent-a-Senior" project will have gotten not only the money you need but all of the publicity you could ever want for your cause as well. This is also the type of project that could lay the groundwork for developing an ongoing nonprofit organization if desired.

NOTE: Before we get to thinking that in order to fund-raise effectively it is necessary to hold an event of some kind, be it a black-tie dance at the Waldorf, a softball game, fashion show, or car wash, let me state that fund-raising is an event in and of itself. Following are some non "event" examples of "Show Me" methodology at work:

Stamp Collecting

The Resistance Stamp Agency, a Palm Beach, Florida, firm that puts out a line of freedom-fighting commemorative stamps, combined stamp collecting and fund-raising when they divided the profits from the sale of stamps in support of Angolan rebels with UNITA (the National Union for the Total Independence of Angola). At $15 for a set of four stamps, the agency sold over 25,000 sets in three months. According to Resistance Agency president Marc Rousso, "We are offering stamps we guarantee will appreciate in value." A tie-in like this provides a simple method of providing a really excellent "Show Me" return on the dollar.

Craft Sales

Once upon a time it was considered illegal for nonprofit organizations to engage in profit-making activities. In the fifties this rule was challenged when public hospitals opened laundries whose profits were used to help fund the operations of the hospital.

Today, most nursing homes in the country operate craft stores in which they sell quilts, Christmas decorations, and other items handmade by the residents, and the profits from which they put back into the home for their services.

Almost any type of handmade items—from baked goods to artwork—especially if fashioned by those who are to be the recipients of the contributions, is sure to be a good lure in our heavily mass-produced society. As the labor is donated, overhead (materials) can be kept very low, and the publicity potential runs high.

Recycling

Over a two-year period in the late seventies, the state of Alaska drastically decreased its funding of nonprofit programs. The Women's Support Network of Anchorage survived this crisis by opening up a store that featured recycled clothes. The used clothing was donated to the organization (allowing for a tax deduction to the donators) and sold for a 100 percent profit to the Women's Network. Today, this store now totally supports a number of the organization's activities, including day care, a twenty-four-hour crisis line, a resource library, and a wide variety of seminars and classes.

Selling recycled, donated items—be they books, records, toys, furniture, or what have you—on a one-shot or ongoing basis again has the advantage of low (or no) overhead and is always an extremely popular, personally satisfying fundraiser for everyone participating in it.

Inscriptions

Even the National Park Service is making an appeal for private contributions. To replenish the cherry trees surrounding the Tidal Basin in our nation's capital, the Park Service is offering to inscribe donors' names in an "official tree directory" for every gift of $150. (Half the price of the trees was donated "in-kind" to the Park Service in return for P.R. for the greenhouse.) Confidence in people's desire to have their names live on in history has led the Park Service to predict a 250-tree (or $37,500) donation by next spring.

Ego gratification is an important consideration in "Show Me" methodology. Throughout the fund-raising process this fact should be kept in mind. Knowing that one's name will appear (for all to see) on the theater seat, hospital wing, or athletic uniform one has paid for goes a long way in enticing some potential donors.

Raffles

Raffles have long been successful examples of "Show Me" methodology in action. With in-kind contributions of appealing goods or services for prizes and a minimal amount of paperwork, raffles are a sure draw, quite easy to conduct, and they usually bring in quite lucrative results. Raffles can be held in conjunction with a special event or as part of a direct-mail campaign. They range from the very simple and straightforward:

First Response Team of Scandia Valley
FUND-RAISER

Win a Goldstar VCR ($300 Value)
Drawing on June 29, 1986, at the Friendly Inn
Live Music—Dancing

Donation $1.00 or 6 for $5.00
Need Not Be Present to Win!

to the more sophisticated and complex:

The New York Public Library

Fifth Avenue & 42nd Street, New York, N.Y. 10018

"Such stuff as dreams are made on. . ."

Dear Friend,

Only Shakespeare could conjure up the perfect description for the unforgettable experiences and magnificent prizes that can be yours in the 1986 FRIENDS OF THE LIBRARY RAFFLE.

Just look through the enclosed brochure . . .

* A sun-filled vacation for two in the tropical paradise of Tahiti . . .
* An exquisite pair of diamond, emerald and onyx earrings from Van Cleef and Arpels . . .
* A champagne flight for five high in the sky over New York aboard the Goodyear Blimp . . .

and dozens of other fabulous prizes you've only dreamed of . . . *until now.*

This spectacular raffle will benefit New York's best-loved cultural institution—The New York Public Library—a place where dreams do come true. Within its marble walls, Chester Carlson dreamed of xerography and changed the way the world does business . . . Edwin Land conceived of instant pictures and the Polaroid camera was born . . . Rachel Carson researched *Silent Spring* and launched the environmental movement . . . and thousands of others—scholars, inventors, performers and entrepreneurs—have found the facts, the figures, the *inspiration* they were seeking.

To make certain that this incomparable cultural resource survives and thrives for the "dreamers" of today and tomorrow, *we need your help.* For despite the "public" in our title, only The Branch Libraries receive their primary funding from governmental sources. To protect the pre-eminence and guarantee the survival of the treasures of The Research Libraries, we must depend on contributions and friends like you.

Your contribution to the FRIENDS OF THE LIBRARY RAFFLE will provide much needed financial support . . .

—to preserve the hundreds of thousands of aging books and manuscripts in our priceless collections

—to keep up with the information explosion by acquiring tens of thousands of new books and periodicals every year
—to maintain our place as *the source* of one of the most complete and up-to-date collections of research materials on earth
—to serve our mission as the Library of *first* and *last* resort.

So take a moment now to enter our 1986 FRIENDS OF THE LIBRARY RAFFLE. Simply return all twelve entry certificates in the enclosed reply envelope (your entry must be postmarked by June 13, 1986). And include your contribution in support of The New York Public Library. Your gift is especially important now because for every $3 you contribute the National Endowment for the Humanities will give $1 in Federal funds. So please be as generous as you can.

Your support will ensure the Library's place as the source of vital knowledge for millions, this year and in the years to come. My warm thanks for your help.

Sincerely,
Andrew Heiskell
Chairman

P.S. Your gift of $35 or more makes you a Friend of the Library. Friends receive invitations to special events and lectures, discounts on Library publications and gifts, and a free subscription to the Library newsletter.

P.P.S. We make every effort to eliminate duplication in the mailing, but as you know, computers are not as smart as individuals. If you have already received more than one copy of this raffle offer, we apologize. Perhaps you can pass along the extra copy to someone who may wish to particiate in the FRIENDS OF THE LIBRARY RAFFLE.

Raffle '86

I want to be a winner!
Enclosed is my contribution of $______, along with ______ Entry Certificates
Please let me know if I have won a prize. (I know that I do not have to make a contribution to enter the Library Raffle, but that my gift of $35 or more makes me a Friend of the Library.)
I've enclosed an extra gift of $______ because I care about the future of The New York Public Library.

Please use my contribution for
The Research Libraries
The Branch Libraries
Only this Branch

The New York Public Library
Fifth Avenue & 42nd Street
New York, N.Y. 10018

The Friends of The New York Public Library
Raffle '86
Suggested contribution per certificate: $3.00
To enter, detach and mail this Entry Certificate along with entry form at the top of page in envelope provided. Winners will be notified by mail at the address on Certificate. Of course, there is no obligation to make a contribution to enter.
Issued to:
NAME
ADDRESS

The Friends of The New York Public Library
Raffle '86
Suggested contribution per certificate: $3.00
To enter, detach and mail this Entry Certificate along with entry form at the top of page in envelope provided. Winners will be notified by mail at the address on Certificate. Of course, there is no obligation to make a contribution to enter.
Issued to:
NAME
ADDRESS

The Friends of The New York Public Library
Raffle '86
Suggested contribution per certificate: $3.00
To enter, detach and mail this Entry Certificate along with entry form at the top

The Friends of The New York Public Library
Raffle '86
Suggested contribution per certificate: $3.00
To enter, detach and mail this Entry Certificate along with entry form at the top

Special Membership Drives

A national cause that is using the "Show Me" approach to fund-raising is the America's Cup competition. In their effort to bring the race back from Australia to the United States, the U.S. Merchant Marine Academy offered contributors of $30 a newsletter and "honorary crew membership."

In addition, they have enlisted the aid of *Newsweek* as a corporate sponsor, from whom they are getting free full-page national advertising space in the magazine. This is something to try with local papers, TV, and radio stations who might not give money but will give advertising space or airtime.

And what about that "honorary crew membership?" A cornerstone of "Show Me" fund-raising is the special membership. People like to feel a part of something. "Membership" is one of the hallowed words in our language. It is also an easy way to give something back for a contribution. To give away membership is usually not very demanding in terms of dollars or time. At the same time, however, membership means responsibility. The people who have paid to be members of your organization are now part of what you are trying to do. That means that you owe them even more than you do a "straight" contributor.

Following is a step-by-step approach to planning and carrying out a successful membership drive that should be applicable, with slight modification, to most of your fund-raising needs:

Step One: Discuss with your board and/or your volunteers the pros and cons of developing a membership, including:

PROS

A large "base of support" in the form of membership will help you add to your shopping and mailing lists.

Everyone is impressed with an idea that has many members behind it. By boosting your image and enhancing your credibility in this way, membership can ultimately aid you in all your other fund-raising efforts.

Membership will supply you with a larger group of supporters who might also lend a hand as well as lending their money and their names to your cause.

Word-of-mouth support for your efforts will be enlarged by having a visible membership.

CONS

You'll need to provide members with a substantial "reward" for their involvement.

Membership usually connotates a vote in the activity of the organization, so you probably will need to develop bylaws. (A weekly or monthly meeting to talk over and decide on organizational matters or simply a once a year election to select board or steering committee members should be acceptable.)

In any case, you can expect to devote some time with members, whether in formal meetings, one to one, or on the phone.

Step Two: If you decide to develop a membership, you need to set up a numerical goal and a timeline to reach that goal. If you decide to have more than one class of membership (in order both to include more people and to get larger membership donations), you also need to work out what that means in terms of what you expect from each class of member and what you will give to each. Here are some typical examples of membership groupings:

SPONSORING MEMBER

An individual or company that gives quite a bit more than the minimum membership fee. Their names should be listed as sponsors of the organization on any printed matter or publicity that is sent out. Perhaps there will be a special table at your special event that will be for sponsors only, special quarterly luncheons, and so on.

CONTRIBUTING MEMBER

Someone who gives you at least a little more than the minimum fee required for membership.

MEMBER

Someone who gives the minimum fee required for membership.

WORKING MEMBER

People who are not in a position to give money, but who will give their time and services on a regular basis (an excellent way of developing a permanent reliable volunteer pool).

Step Three: Prepare your materials. Usually a membership brochure with a tear-off form works well. If you call this form an application, people have a tendency to be more eager to join. The facing page shows a sample form from the Second Stage Theater in New York:

Make this into a self-mailer so that you can do a separate mailing for membership independent of your general fund drive.

Step Four: Get everyone involved with your organization, including yourself, to be a member. Just as in doing general fund-raising, it is easier to sign up members when you are able to say that you have 100 percent participation of everyone involved with the organization.

Step Five: Have a definite kickoff to your membership drive. If your goals are high enough to warrant it, you might hold

How to contribute your money:

At THE SECOND STAGE, there are Tangible expressions of gratitude for every level of giving. All contributions are tax-deductible. And may be charged to major credit cards.

____ $5 Free Second Stage button.
____ $10 Free button. Advance play notification.
____ $25 The Above. Plus Free "Not Your Ordinary Theatre-Goer" T-Shirt.
____ $50 The Above. Plus Free Second Stage Tote Bag.
____ $75 The Above. Plus two free tickets to a matinee.
____ $100 All of the above benefits. Plus your name in the program.

THE BIG TIME

To convey our extreme gratitude to contributors to our operational expenses, we have established categories of special benefits. These contributors receive priority seating, special invitations to select events, their name in the program. And these extras:

____ SPONSOR	$150–499	Two tickets to each production.
____ PATRON	$500–999	Two tickets for Opening Night performances and receptions.
____ BENEFACTOR	$1000–2999	Four tickets for Opening Night performances and receptions.
____ ANGEL	$3000 up	Four tickets for Opening Night. Two tickets to all the Big Parties.

MAKE THEATRE HISTORY

Donations to the McGinn/Cazale Theatre Fund can create a lasting testimony to your generosity.

____ $1000 Your name, or any name of your choosing, engraved on an audience chair.
____ $5000 Your name, or any name of your choosing, engraved on the Capital Benefactors' Plaque in the Lobby.

NAME____________________
ADDRESS____________________
PHONE (DAY)____________ (NIGHT)________
____CHECK enclosed. (Make payable to THE SECOND STAGE)
____ American Express____ Visa____ Master Card
Account#____________ Expiration Date____
Signature____________________
(FILL OUT, DETACH, GIVE TO THE HOUSE MANAGER)
Or mail to THE SECOND STAGE, P.O. Box 1807, Ansonia Station, NYC, 10023

some type of event to get things rolling. In any case, put out a press release. Be very clear about your objectives and your timeline for the membership drive, i.e., "By September we need to have 100 members interested in helping us get to Washington, D.C.!"

If you have a large number of members, you may want to issue membership cards. Below is the "Associate Member" card from the American Museum of Natural History. Note how the museum cleverly and efficiently uses the issuance of this card to accomplish a variety of purposes:

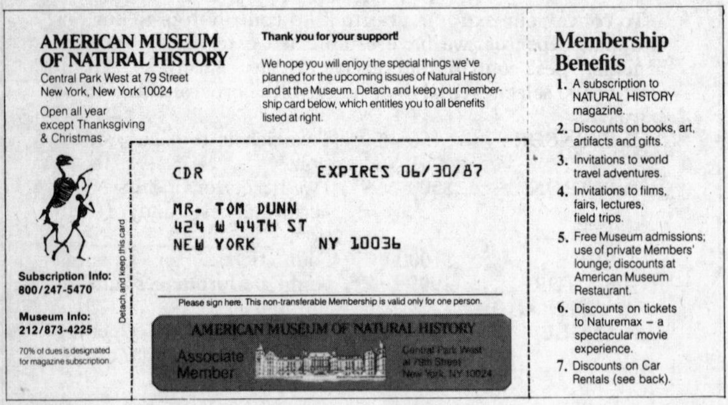

AMERICAN MUSEUM OF NATURAL HISTORY
Central Park West at 79 Street
New York, New York 10024

Open all year except Thanksgiving & Christmas

Subscription Info: 800/247-5470

Museum Info: 212/873-4225

70% of dues is designated for magazine subscription

Thank you for your support!

We hope you will enjoy the special things we've planned for the upcoming issues of Natural History and at the Museum. Detach and keep your membership card below, which entitles you to all benefits listed at right.

Detach and keep this card

CDR EXPIRES 06/30/87

MR. TOM DUNN
424 W 44TH ST
NEW YORK NY 10036

Please sign here. This non-transferable Membership is valid only for one person.

AMERICAN MUSEUM OF NATURAL HISTORY
Associate Member
Central Park West at 79th Street New York, NY 10024

Membership Benefits

1. A subscription to NATURAL HISTORY magazine.
2. Discounts on books, art, artifacts and gifts.
3. Invitations to world travel adventures.
4. Invitations to films, fairs, lectures, field trips.
5. Free Museum admissions; use of private Members' lounge; discounts at American Museum Restaurant.
6. Discounts on tickets to Naturemax – a spectacular movie experience.
7. Discounts on Car Rentals (see back).

Step Six: Make sure that at least once a year you hold some type of event for members. It can be a separate "members only" event, or this event can be combined with a special fund-raising event open to the general public, in which members get special privileges, such as preferred seating, a pre- or post-event cocktail party with the guests of honor, and so on. Whatever it is, make sure that it is something that is enjoyable and will leave a good feeling in people's minds about their involvement with your group.

Step Seven: Conduct mid-year evaluations of your membership program. Ask yourself the following questions:

1. What are our members getting for their membership that they wouldn't get if they were simply contributors?

2. Is our membership increasing at a healthy rate?

3. Who are our members and why have they joined? (Sometimes people feel they have fulfilled their obligation by joining at the minimum rate where they might otherwise have given a larger amount as a contribution.)

4. Are our overall goals being met by having members? Should we continue the program? (Or is membership taking too much staff and volunteer time? Too much money?)

* * *

NOTE: Membership is not appropriate for every fund-raising project. A onetime project like the ice skating rink definitely doesn't need to bother gathering members. A project that has a chance of growing into an ongoing nonprofit organization might want to consider developing a membership, as any ongoing program membership can well become the backbone of its future support.

The organization I currently work with has had several different types of membership programs in effect for many years. Although its $25 per year "contributing membership" was beneficial in the past, the last five years' fund-raising efforts have grown to a point where the usefulness of this type of membership no longer exists. We found that we were spending more to service members—answering questions about membership itself, printing up membership brochures, and so on—than we were bringing in from these members. This year we finally dropped what had become, for us, an outmoded mode of fund-raising.

Membership might be a very good method of fund-raising—and even more importantly sometimes, of image building—for your organization. Don't be afraid to involve others in your idea; just be sure you first spend time thinking about membership in terms of the resources and goals of your organization and then plan for it before you jump in and offer it.

Advertising Space Sales

Another important adjunct to "Show Me" fund-raising is selling advertising space. Hopefully, you will be able to get the printing of your event's program donated. (More about how to do that in Chapter 4.) If for some reason you can't, or even if you can, it is always worthwhile to sell advertising space in the journal of the day's events.

First, compile various advertising solicitation target lists consisting of the following:

1. Friendly vendors (companies your organization does regular business with, i.e., your office supply store, hardware store, building exterminator, and so on).
2. Neighbors (shops, banks, restaurants, and other businesses located near your organization and/or near the site of your upcoming event).
3. Personal contacts (board members', volunteers', and staff's business contacts—and board members' businesses as well).
4. Business contributors (businesses that have given money to your organization in the past).
5. Businesses that are known to give to organizations or causes such as yours.
6. Friends (businesses, organizations, and individuals associated with your guest of honor who may want to put in a "congratulations" or "greetings" type ad).

Of course, every time you sell ad space after the initial time, the first group to hit is those who previously bought space.

Write an ad solicitation letter that includes background information about your organization, your event, and the projected audience (in numbers) that will see the program.

Then tailor each letter to the specific target group to whom it is being sent, i.e., your letter to "Friendly vendors" will talk about how you've enjoyed doing business with them for so many years; your letter to a board contact will be signed by that board member. Here's a sample of an advertising solicitation letter to businesses that serve your clientele:

April 14, 1987

Dear__________:

Our 1987 Senior Sense 10th Anniversary Luncheon Program will be seen by over 5,000 senior citizens and their family members.

To help pay for the printing of this publication, we need to sell several pages of ads. This is a great opportunity for your organization to reach a large part of our community's active senior citizen population.

We hope you'll consider buying an ad for our 1987 program. Ad rates and deadline information appear on the attached insertion order form.

Thank you for supporting Senior Sense.

Sincerely,

A. Elder,
Director

Enclosures:

1. If possible, a mock-up of the program (or last year's program if this is a repeat).
2. An insertion order form, as below:

Senior Sense 10th Anniversary Luncheon
April 14, 1987
Journal Advertising Insertion Order

Yes, we would like to place an advertisement in the Senior Sense 10th Anniversary Luncheon Journal. Our space preference is checked below.

______	Full page	\$300	Size 4⅞″ (w) × 7¾″ (h)
______	Half page	\$200	Size 4⅞″ (w) × 3¾″ (h)
______	Quarter page	\$150	Size 2 5/16″ (w) × 3¾″ (h)

Closing dates: March 1—Insertion orders and "Pub-Set" copy
March 23—Camera-ready Material

Name:______________________________
Address:____________________________
Phone:______________________________
Signature:___________________________
Copy Instructions:____________________
____
____

Please send invoice and checking copy to attention of:
____

Please return to: Senior Sense
2820 East Fourth Avenue
Columbus, Ohio
Attention: Wendy Paul

If you can enlist an artist—or very often the printer—to create an ad for those clients that don't have one, you'll fare far better with some smaller stores or businesses that may not have a prepared ad but have a logo or a business card that could be made into an ad. Make sure you get clear closing dates from the printer and/or artist as to when they need the material from the client. Be sure to send the solicitation letters out well in advance of these dates (usually sixty days prior, at least).

As far as pricing the ads, check on the going rate for publications in your community and develop a rate sheet based on the number of people who will see the ad and the fact that it's a charitable contribution. Charging whatever you think the traffic will bear is fine, but if response is slow, you may have overcalculated your market. In that case try offering a page of business card ads, each one-eighth of a page and thus, half of the one-quarter-page price. This tactic works very well as it gives businesses who never have enough in their budget to do any advertising the opportunity to do some.

Within a week after you put the ad solicitation letters in the mail, have your volunteers start follow-up calls. Call *every single* name on your lists that has not yet sent in an insertion order. Ideally, follow up these phone calls with an in-person visit within three weeks and, if needed, a reminder call within six weeks.

The time to bill your clients for their ads is when the program is printed. Send out the invoices along with a tear sheet of their ad or an entire copy of the program with their ad paper clipped.

If you end up with the happy dilemma of having sold more ads than your space permits, consider adding on pages. Advertising space sales can be a very lucrative "Show Me" technique that can cover the costs of your program production and much more. It can transform a marginally profitable event into a moneymaker, especially if a printer and typesetter can be enlisted to donate their services.

In addition to selling ads for special events programs, if your group has any type of ongoing performances or talks or sporting events, don't pass up the opportunity to sell ad space for the season in programs for these as well.

When creating "Show Me" methods for your organization, don't be afraid to borrow or steal an idea. Finding out through the media what other people are doing and have done is very helpful in coming up with ideas for your organization. Borrowing the concept for a fund-raising method from another source is an accepted and valuable part of the fund-raising process. As an example, the block association in the neighborhood where I work started a Saturday afternoon film series last year as a way to raise $20 to $30 a week and also give the neighborhood children an activity to do together.

I'm taking that idea and turning it into a "Meet the Writer" film series with a goal of $1,500. My audience—i.e., givers—will not take away from their audience, as all I've borrowed is their concept and altered it to meet my quite separate purposes.

As long as any idea hasn't been overdone (and you'll get a sense of this through your research), it is still a worthwhile idea. It is best still to come up with your own original idea, which may not be as hard as it may sound. Ideas come to people at strange times. Keep a notebook and pen on you at all times—in your pocket or purse and beside your bed—in which to keep track of ideas. Note ideas from all sources—this book, another book, the newspaper, a planning meeting, dream, whatever. Ask people within and outside of your group for their suggestions. Everyone has heard a "cute" or novel idea on how to raise money, how to give something to people for what they give to you. Save your lists of ideas that strike your fancy—if they don't seem right for your first fund-raising effort, they might be workable in the future.

* * *

There is no way of *knowing* which method is right for you (i.e., absolutely foolproof, guaranteed to succeed). However, the selection of appropriate technique does not come out of any magical or mystical process. As I've tried to show in this chapter, detailed analysis of your organization's resources, goals, and audience should ensure a well-thought-out decision-making process that leads to a choice of potentially profitable fund-raising methods.

The "magic" of fund-raising, that intangible that makes some drives succeed while others don't, has much to do with selecting the appropriate method. Unless you have chosen a fund-raising method that is totally inappropriate for your audience (i.e., a $500 per ticket benefit when the average size of your donations is $25), you will be successful if you plan well. If you set a realistic goal, work out a timeline to achieve that goal that gives you numerous chances to analyze how you are doing and make any necessary revisions as you go along, you will be successful. Let's move on to our next chapter—planning—the key to successful fund-raising.

Resource List: Chapter 3

Now we're getting into the nuts and bolts of this business. Here are some suggestions for more in-depth study:

New Ventures
several publications available at
251 Park Avenue South, Twelfth Floor
New York, New York 10010

The Art of Patronage
special edition of
Horizon Magazine
P.O. Drawer 30
Tuscaloosa, Alabama 35401

chapter 4

PLANNING

People give to people, not to publications . . .
—Late twentieth-century fund-raising maxim

Now that you have set clearly defined goals and have chosen the project and methods to meet them, it is time to organize. The importance of well-thought-out detailed planning cannot be overemphasized. It is truly the "make or break" stage of your entire fund-raising effort. It needn't be overwhelming, however. Following methodical step-by-step activities, the planning process will be painless and complete.

Volunteers

The first step in this planning process is to marshal your forces—to enlist the aid of people to help you put the project into operation. If you're like 87 percent of the nonprofit organizations in this country, you do not have a paid fund-raiser on your staff. And due to limited resources, most nonprofits are already understaffed (and overworked) in every area of operation. Thus, volunteer help is an absolute essential.

If your organization currently has no volunteers or fewer than you need (and for a fund-raising project, you'll probably need as many as you can get and you'll need them *now*), don't despair. Getting people to volunteer their time, skills, and services can be easy if you employ the "Show Me" philosophy. What you may offer them will vary, depending upon the type and scope of your organization, but every organization has something: free tickets, free classes, refreshments, college credits, social and business contacts, camaraderie, a sense of aiding a good cause, T-shirts, buttons, membership, and so on.

How do these potential volunteers find out about these benefits awaiting them in return for their time? Advertise. Using the "Show Me" approach, offer your local newspaper a credit in your project program in return for free advertising space. Give them enough lead time and most local papers will be happy to allow you to place an ad where they have "blank" (unsold) space. And even if you don't get donated space, it won't cost more than $10 to run a want ad. A motivating and eye-catching ad could be along these lines:

> IS THE FATE OF OUR YOUTH IMPORTANT TO YOU?
> Will you consider giving one night a week for a month to help make this community a better place for our youth to live? Come next Tuesday to find out why we need you! (Give address, phone number, and time.)

Unless your ad comes out the day of the worst blizzard in the twentieth century (as happened to me a few years ago in Minneapolis), you will get response to an announcement such as this. Now, what to do with that response. . . . On the night of the informational meeting have all the printed matter (brochures, articles, a typewritten prospectus you've drawn up) about your organization ready to pass out with enough copies to go around.

Again, the "Show Me" technique can get free refreshments for your meeting to make it more pleasant. Using the same approach as with the local paper, and, again, making this approach far enough in advance, most local grocery stores will help out with cookies and soft drinks.

Develop a workable volunteer information form to bring to the meeting with the necessary contact information and a variety of jobs from which the prospective volunteer can choose. Word these job responsibilities in a low-key nonthreatening way: Don't ask if a potential volunteer wants to "fund-raise" or "contribute." Your purpose is to interest recruits, not scare people off. Below is a suggested form:

Sample Volunteer Information Form

Name:________________________________
Address:______________________________
________________________ Zip:________
Phone: (day)________________ (eve.)________
Best time to call:________________________
I am interested in volunteering my time to do:
phone calling_____
typing_____
talking about organization_____
using my special skills (please list)____________
____
anything______________________________

At the meeting itself you or another member of your organization can talk about your goals for the project and the reasons behind them. Keep this talk brief and allow plenty of time for questions and suggestions. Be very direct about the fact that you need volunteers and discuss the different types of help that are needed. Don't collect the volunteer information forms until this discussion is over because often, people will wait to hear more about a particular type of volunteer work before deciding to jump in and sign up. This also gives you a chance to make each of the jobs sound attractive. The point of this informational meeting is to get yourself a good list of interested volunteers. Don't have this meeting go on too long and don't try to accomplish everything at this first meeting. Encourage people to sign up and then do get back to them promptly about the next meeting. Make your volunteer fund-raisers feel special!

It's important to give your volunteers as much (if not more!) respect and attention as you would your paid staff. Preparations for volunteer meetings must be as carefully worked out as for any other type of meeting. For the first official working meeting of your volunteer committee, type up an agenda and get that agenda to your volunteers before the meeting date. Even if the only items on the agenda are as follows, it's helpful to everyone to know what will be discussed and how much time is allotted to each topic.

Agenda for First Volunteer Meeting

1. *Introductions:* Everyone, including you and any staff you may have, should participate in these three-to-five-minute-per-person intros that should include each person's reasons for being here.

2. *Introduction to the Problem:* Take twenty minutes to a half hour to do for your volunteers what you'll continually be doing throughout your fund-raising efforts—state your case. (Bring copies of notes, articles, facts and figures, letters of support from well-known people, and so on to support your talk.)

3. *Open Discussion of Possible Solutions:* Let everyone participate in a thirty-to-forty-minute discussion of what could and should be done. This brainstorming session is a great way to come up with "Show Me" methods and will also give everyone a chance to express themselves. Be prepared with information on potential costs, realistic goals, and so on and make sure the basic problem remains the focal point of the possible solutions.

4. *Division of Responsibilities—Committees:* Ask anyone to get involved with nonprofit planning, and they will oftentimes grumble, "Not more committee meetings." All the platitudes and old jokes about trying to design a camel by committee and the like are not without some validity, yet here I am recommending that the most constructive way to work with people on a project such as a fund-raising drive is to develop committees. Let me take a moment to explain why I am fond of the committee structure for volunteer fund-raising:

a. Committees help to spread the burden of responsibility. By having committees that are each in charge of a specific part (or parts) of a project, no one person ends up having to shoulder all the work. Endless marathon planning sessions are also avoided, as committees can work more efficiently, and effectively, due to their smaller numbers and only need report back to the entire group for feedback and approvals.

b. Committees make better use of each person's specific area of expertise. Instead of dividing up a drive into its three parts (i.e., direct mail, luncheon, and door-to-door) for committees, if you have two or three people who are skilled in bookkeeping, say, it can be very helpful to organize them into a finance committee that can take care of preliminary budget drafting, monitor activities, and report back to the rest of the group.

c. Committees help get and keep people involved. There is nothing worse for morale or for the ultimate outcome of your project than to use your volunteers only for the "slave labor" tasks (stuffing envelopes, putting up posters, and so on) that are part of every fund-raising drive. Let your volunteers know that they're bringing skills and expertise that you want to use. The committee structure is a great way to give a person who is volunteering time with you (or is employed by you) a sense that he or she is an integral part of the overall effort, not just another envelope stuffer.

It is very important to instill a sense of personal responsibility in everyone working on the project. In addition to forming committees, select a chairperson to head each committee so it's not always a case of your giving orders and their following them. Play toward people's strengths—choose someone with some experience in the committee's activity or with a willingness to learn. A volunteer who has worked in personnel, say, might be an excellent chairperson of the "Rent-a-Senior" week organizational committee. Also, be sure to choose chairpeople who work well with other people—they too must understand how important it is that each committee member feel worthwhile and appreciated.

ONE WORD OF CAUTION: The biggest obstacle to success facing most nonprofit organizations is that of becoming "committeed to death." It's all too easy to find that the only real business getting accomplished in your organization is committee business—i.e., keeping members apprised of meetings, writing up and circulating minutes, agendas, and so on. Be careful not to let the committee system overpower the main function of your group. If this seems to be happening, sit down and reassess the way you're operating to see if in fact you are losing sight of your goal of raising funds to meet your need. Always remember that the individuals who are donating their time to you have to be treated with respect and dignity.

5. *Making Assignments:* Specific goals for each person should be set out in the last five minutes of the meeting so that everyone leaves knowing what to do next (i.e., coming to the special event brainstorming session, going to the direct-mail drive planning meeting, getting letters to sign, getting lists of people with whom to follow up, and so on. Give everyone a "contact" sheet to fill out before the next meeting. This will be the basis of the shopping list for the drive.

At each planning meeting, be sure to set aside some time for discussion of any questions and/or problems people may have about the goal, the drive, the methods, the plan, and so on. It is always best to test ideas out with your committee first. Whether it be the contents of a letter or a door-to-door "pitch," try it out on your committee before spending time and money on what might be an ineffective approach.

At the close of every planning meeting, review what has been accomplished so far. Make your committee members feel good about their work so they'll leave feeling enthusiastic about the next stage. Along with giving each committee member a specific task(s), be sure to express your thanks for their efforts.

And before discussing the actual planning of the fund-raising drive, I want to stress the importance and value of volunteers to the non-profit fund-raising world by sharing three profiles of people whose volunteered time and talents are, indeed, priceless:

* * *

Waring Jones is one of those rare individuals who has both the time and the resources to assist organizations and ideas that he feels are important. Born in Minneapolis, he has lived his whole life in the Midwest and contributes his time and skills to a diverse number of nonprofit groups in the area, including the Outward Bound School, the Playwrights' Center, and the Jack London Society. He's been known to dress up in a gorilla suit and stand on the street as a living billboard for a twenty-four-hour marathon fund-raiser (that almost made the *Guinness Book of Records*—a great way to get extra publicity for your event, by the way, even if you don't actually make it into the book).

Waring also understands the business of the nonprofit world and how our laws are structured to benefit groups. In the case of a theater in Minneapolis that was facing severe money problems, he arranged to buy the building from them and then lease it back at a dollar a year for ninety-nine years. (This becomes a wonderful tax write-off and a great way for a nonprofit group to be in control of a building without having to deal with the problems that accompany actual ownership.)

Waring is an example of a volunteer who stays interested in helping nonprofits because he enjoys himself. This is a key idea to remember in working with volunteers: Make sure they are having fun.

* * *

Phyllis Lambert is a Canadian architect, writer, photographer, and dedicated urban preservationist. Deeply concerned about the quality of urban life, in 1975 she formed Heritage Montreal, a citizens' group that is committed to restoring and protecting the old buildings and neighborhoods in Montreal. Under Phyllis's leadership, the group has been successful in raising over $20 million in government grants and loans to turn commercial development efforts into a housing cooperative for inner city residents. Phyllis is also founder of the Canadian Center for Architecture, a $17.5 million museum and study center devoted to the art of architecture. Working sixteen-hour days, contributing large sums of her own to these projects, Phyllis Lambert is a full-time volunteer equipped with unique vision, expertise, and incredible energy.

* * *

Amy Lynn gets my vote as the most valuable volunteer fund-raiser in New York City. She is the master of arranging special events and should get credit for being the master planner of fund-raising. The wife of an entertainment lawyer, Amy never accepts a salary for what she does. She gives of her time and skills to the very largest institutions, such as Lincoln Center, and to the small groups, such as mine. One of her pet projects is the Museum of the City of New York's annual library sale. Various memorabilia from the library's collection are offered in what is one of the bargain fund-raising events of the year in New York. Amy works with a staff of volunteers and runs this sale in a manner that would make the president of Sears Roebuck envious.

The importance of exact scheduling, precise list-making, and cultivation of solid, up-to-date potential donor-mailing lists to the planning process of any fund-raising campaign cannot be overemphasized. Amy Lynn not only has great knowledge, expertise, and experience in these areas, but is willing to work to set up these systems and teach other volunteers and staff members how to use them.

The key to working with a volunteer like Amy is to make sure that she is getting good support for her ideas and time. For instance, she is wonderful at organizing a mailing list that will bring results, but you have to respect her time (as you should with any volunteer) and make sure that the mailing list is kept clean and ready to be used in her absence. The first time a volunteer spends an afternoon redoing work that should have been done before he or she arrived is when you start to lose that volunteer.

A Timeline: Press Releases, Direct-mail Campaigns, Door-to-door Drives, "Free" Concerts

An essential preliminary step in the planning process for every fund-raising project is to set down a timeline. Map out a rough schedule of what needs to be accomplished by when and try to stick to this schedule as closely as possible. The benefits of this kind of groundwork are immeasurable. Having a timeline ensures that no aspect of the project will be overlooked. It gives everyone a clear idea of what is expected of him and allows him to budget his own time to accomplish his particular tasks by the assigned due dates. Use your timeline as a guide for achieving maximum effect with each step along the way to your goal.

Let's develop a timeline and pass the steps we will take

to raise funds to build the ice skating rink, using a direct-mail campaign and hosting an on-site wrap-up rink party.

Press Releases

We'll need to announce your campaign with a press release, let's say on October 1, since your committee has decided potential donors will feel more generous around Christmastime. You'll also want to launch your direct-mail campaign, then have follow-up phone calling and finish with a party at the ice skating rink before your final deadline of December 1. Let's look at these steps in greater detail.

Direct-Mail Campaigns

OCTOBER 1:

1. Send out a simple press release announcing the kickoff of the drive to local print media.

Sample Press Release

October 1, 1987 Contact: Don Brinker
555-1215

For Immediate Release

Langford to Have Ice Skating Rink

The Action for Youth Committee, a group of Langford citizens concerned with providing safe and productive recreational activities for the young people of Langford, is trying to raise funds to build an ice skating rink on the corner of Broadway and Dodge to be in use by this coming winter.

According to committee chairperson Don Brinker: "The people of Langford—children, teenagers, and adults—really don't have much in the way of outdoor recreation available to them in the wintertime. The ice skating rink will change all that."

We need to raise $5,500 by December 1 to have the rink in operation by this winter. Action for Youth has already received $1,000 from the Langford City Council, and the

XYZ Construction Company, contractors for the project, has agreed to donate $1,000 of the rink building costs to the project.

To raise the remaining $3,500, Action for Youth is currently conducting a mail campaign that will be followed by a wrap-up party for the community to be held on the site of the proposed rink on November 24.

To help put Langford "on the ice," contributions should be sent to: Action for Youth Committee, 245 West River Road, Langford, Illinois 12745.

2. Send out copy that can be used as a public service announcement (a message broadcast free of charge as a service to the community) to local TV and radio stations.

Sample Public Service Announcement

October 1, 1987 Contact Don Brinker
555-1215

Time: Thirty seconds

What would you rather have your children doing on a crisp winter's afternoon? Watching yet another 1950s TV rerun or perfecting their figure eights on Langford's new ice skating rink?

If you're as tired of the winter doldrums as we are, the Action for Youth Committee brings good news. They are trying to raise $3,500 from the people of Langford to build an ice skating rink right here in our town. If they meet their goal by December 1, we can all be on the ice by this coming winter. So, all you Hans Brinkers—and parents of Hans Brinkers—out there, please help put Langford on the ice and send as much as you can as soon as you can to: Action for Youth Committee, 245 West River Road, Langford, Illinois 12745.

* * *

NOTE: Be sure to include the address where checks can be sent on both the press release and public service announcement, as well as a contact name and phone number of someone in your organization who is available and knowledgeable to answer any questions about the project.

A few days after these mailings, follow up with a phone call. Confirm that they have received the material and ask if you can answer any questions they might have. These phone calls can serve to get your release off the bottom of the pile and into print or on the air.

3. Send out the letters of appeal.

There are tens of thousands of samples of direct-mail letters that incorporate a wide variety of styles and approaches. In keeping with the creative spirit of the new fund-raising, I'd like to share with you a fund-raising letter that illustrates the kind of dialogue with prospective donors that we are trying to develop. In Chapter 2 we discussed how difficult it would be for a new musical group to get started, given today's governmental funding picture. This letter is from an organization in Manhattan that provides low-cost performance space to new music, dance, and theatrical groups and is doing a wonderful job of creative fund-raising:

SYMPHONY SPACE

A NOT-FOR-PROFIT COMMUNITY-SPONSORED CENTER FOR THE PERFORMING ARTS

Dear Friend,
We're looking for backers. Wanna be an angel? Here's a new script.

"NINETY-FIFTH STREET"

A Real-Life Drama in One Significant Act

(LIGHTS COME UP ON A CONCERNED NEW YORKER opening yet another piece of direct mail advertising. MUSIC UNDER: "The Unfinished Symphony")

CONCERNED NEW YORKER

(Reads:)
"We'd like you to consider becoming a member of Symphony Space."
(sighs:)

Who's got the time? What's Symphony Space?

(Suddenly, as if by magic, a STILL, SMALL VOICE is heard)

STILL, SMALL VOICE

Wait! Don't throw away that expensive mailing piece. You know, you really should become a member . . .

CONCERNED NEW YORKER

I should? Why?

STILL, SMALL VOICE

Symphony Space is a place where they do all kinds of things in music, theatre, dance, film, and literature. They are very interesting. And exciting. And innovative. And inexpensive . . . sometimes free.

CONCERNED NEW YORKER

Good! Whenever they have something I'm interested in, I'll buy tickets and go. Why do I have to bother about membership?

STILL, SMALL VOICE

(MUSIC SEGUES: "Pathetique Symphony")

They really need you. What they've accomplished is remarkable, but did you know they have to raise a vast percentage of their budget through contributions?

CONCERNED NEW YORKER

How come? Why don't they just charge more for tickets?

STILL, SMALL VOICE

(getting more impassioned)

They can't do that! Symphony Space has been devoted to providing New Yorkers with excellent artistic events at the *lowest* possible prices. They've helped to revitalize the Upper West Side community. They've given a break to countless numbers of minority artists. And have served all kinds of performing groups who use the place at the most advantageous subsidized rental rates.

CONCERNED NEW YORKER

(growing interested)

Oh, Symphony Space does all that?

STILL, SMALL VOICE

That's one part of it. Symphony Space also creates their own wonderful events. They invented the Wall-to-Wall free marathon concert and created Wall-to-Wall Bach, Beethoven, Schubert, Copland, Cage and Rodgers, among others.

CONCERNED NEW YORKER

Oh yeah . . . I've heard about those. Thousands of people waiting on line in the street to get in.

STILL, SMALL VOICE

Not if they're members! *They* receive priority admission to all free events. Why not become a member today and take advantage of all their membership benefits. Why are you hesitating?

CONCERNED NEW YORKER

(agitated)

I just want to be sure that I'll be doing something significant with my money. Something that will make a difference.

STILL, SMALL VOICE

Oh, you will be! Membership support opens up doors for further funding from foundations, corporations, and the government. Why, it's a vote of confidence for one of the good things in life!

(MUSIC CRESCENDO: "New World Symphony")

CONCERNED NEW YORKER

(inspired)

O.K., I'll do it! This will be . . . my SIGNIFICANT ACT!

(THEY embrace and send in their membership forms as the MUSIC SWELLS and the)

LIGHTS FADE

How about it?

Allan Miller   Isaiah Sheffer
Artistic Directors

Whether the communication is actually in dialogue form, as it is in this letter, or in a more traditional letter style, this awareness of *who* you are writing to and what that person's concerns, questions, and attitudes are is essential. You must know who it is you are asking for money and appeal to that person's characteristics. If you simply write into a void—to that anonymous mass, the contributors—you won't be able to press the right buttons that will get you what you want.

Develop a personality profile of the typical person you are

trying to reach. Ask yourself, or better yet, ask your volunteers: What does he or she like? Dislike? What does he find important? Exciting? Meaningful? *Personally*. Remember, in the new "Show Me" fund-raising, we are providing personal rewards for giving to our public concerns.

In addition to this reader-oriented approach, the Symphony Space letter incorporates all the elements necessary for a fund-raising letter to be effective.

Key Elements of a Successful Fund-raising Letter

- Describe the sender.
- Describe the reader.
- Establish the need for help.
- Pinpoint that need (your goal).
- State the project budget.
- Lay out the timeline for the drive.
- Describe how the effectiveness of the drive will be measured.

A Treasury of Successful Appeal Letters provides a sampling of "the best fund-raising letters in the world," along with commentary by their authors. It is available for $49.50 from the Public Service Materials Center, 111 North Central Avenue, Hartsdale, New York 10530. Most public libraries also carry this entertaining reference.

Following is a simple appeal letter, incorporating the seven key elements that might be used for the ice skating rink drive:

> Dear ____________*
>
> It is a documented fact that family tensions and problems tend to increase in the wintertime. As we are cooped up inside together for longer periods of time, we tend to get on each other's nerves. A group of your neighbors and

*Use the person's first name if someone in your organization—board or staff member or volunteer—knows him.

friends has gathered together to help solve the problem of what to do with the children during the winter. We'd like to build an ice skating rink on vacant land that the city has promised to give to us for this purpose (and also to maintain for us once the rink is built).

We are asking 100 friends and prominent members of our community to help us raise $3,500. This $3,500 will allow us to build the ice skating rink. (The city council has already donated $1,000 and the XYZ Construction Company has pledged to donate $1,000 of their fee if we can raise the $3,500.) Our plan is to have this money raised and construction started by December 1, so we can use the ice skating rink this winter.

At a party on the site of the new ice rink on November 24, the Saturday after Thanksgiving, we'll announce the names of contributors who have helped us reach our goal and affix a plaque on the site listing these names as well. As a special thank-you to everyone who contributes $50 or more, we will issue lovely enameled pins of the ice skating rink engraved with the year it was built.

Can't we include your name among this group? (Enclosed is a self-addressed envelope for your donation.)

Thank you for considering this request. We will all know we've been successful in our campaign as we see the youth of our community (and some of the adults as well) using our new outdoor ice skating rink made possible by your interest in the welfare of our community!

Sincerely,

Make sure the letter is signed either by someone who knows the reader/prospect personally or by a well-known personality who is enlisted for this drive for the purpose of using his or her name. (A sports celebrity would be especially appropriate, considering the goal. A local politician or TV or radio personality also always helps focus attention and ensure a better response.)

Another very effective tool that can be used in small mailings like the ice skating rink campaign is to encourage people to write a personal note to their acquaintances on the letters they sign. Every "Susan, I can see little Jessie in the Ice Capades now!" or "Hal, I hope we can count on your always generous support!" can make a big difference. Take it from me, these notes really do work.

Include a contribution card and a self-addressed envelope with each letter to allow the reader to make an immediate response to your request while the full impact of the letter's sentiments is upon him. Making it easier to respond by including the self-addressed envelope makes it more likely that he will respond and also ensures that the check will end up in the proper place.

The contribution card provides a means to keep your mailing list information updated. It also provides an opportunity to analyze your mailing list. Coding your contribution cards with an unobtrusive letter or numeral in one corner, corresponding to a certain category of recipient (such as lawyer, CEO, neighborhood parent), allows you to see where your strengths and weaknesses lie. It will tell you where your strongest areas of support lie and which areas you need to work harder at cultivating.

Sample Contribution Card

Ice Skating Rink Campaign

Name:________________________________
Address:______________________________
________________________ ZIP:________
Phone: (day) __________ (eve.) _____________
Amount of contribution enclosed:
$15 ____ $25 ____ $50 ____ $100 ____ More ____
Thank you!

When economically feasible, it is often helpful to include support materials along with your letters of appeal. A nicely printed brochure or a photocopy of a letter of support you've received or a positive newspaper article on your organization adds to the feeling of professionalism and credibility that you want to establish.

Let me underline that point: YOU WANT TO COMMUNICATE A FEELING OF PROFESSIONALISM IN ORDER TO ESTABLISH CREDIBILITY FOR YOUR ORGANIZATION OR PROJECT. This is very important. Sometimes, newly formed organizations defeat themselves by trying to capitalize on their lack of experience and funds. The logic behind this misinformed fund-raising approach goes something like this:

1. People (or corporations or foundations) will see how inexperienced and poor we are.
2. People will realize how desperately we need their support.
3. Therefore, people will be more motivated to give to us.

In actuality, the typical response to the "poor me" approach follows more along these lines:

1. Boy, these guys are operating on half a shoestring.
2. They are really struggling—looks like they could drop off the face of the earth tomorrow.
3. Therefore, I better not give them anything.

By putting together and putting out a professional confident image, you look like you know what you're doing and like you're going to be around for a while—important considerations for people deciding whether to part with their dollars. This is not to imply that you should go beyond your means and spend a lot of money to create this image. A modest request accompanied by a very expensive brochure is just as much a turn-off to potential investors as a sloppily put together, badly photocopied one.

Invest in good quality letterhead (not wildly expensive, just good) with a well-laid-out logo that isn't too "cute" but says something about what you do (or want to do). The need for zealous proofreading should be obvious. One misspelling can obliterate the effects of your whole campaign.

Work out the timeline well in advance with your typists (for a small mailing) or printer (for a larger mailing). Make sure you know what is expected of you and when; i.e. get the printer's deadline for receiving copy and stationery from you so that the mailing deadline can be met.

It's a good idea to make up a master timetable, including everything from ordering the stationery to the trip to the post office before you begin.

Sample Master Timetable for Ice Skating Rink Mailing of 100 Letters

July 15: Order stationery.
September 1: Copy to printer (including contribution cards and any supplemental materials).

or

September 25: Copy to typists (twenty letters by two people per day = two and a half days).
September 30: Letters and all printed materials ready.
October 1: Mailing Party.

(Almost all public relations firms, printers, or even schools that offer printing or graphic design classes can be approached for logo ideas.)

If your letters are going to be individually hand-typed, make a schedule of how many letters must be done per person per day. (Don't forget that many companies can make memory typewriters or word processors available to your group at night or on weekends when their employees aren't using them.) If you use computerized equipment to print out your letters, try to make them look hand-done. According to *Direction,* a newsletter of Direct Marketing Consultants, in this day of the computerized letter anything you can do to make your letters look individually typed is advantageous. Include everything that would appear on a regular typed letter—such as a date and a secretary's initials. If it's manageable, try to hand write the addresses on the envelopes. Hand-addressed envelopes tend to be opened much more readily and their contents viewed in a more positive light than those done by machine.

When all of your mailing pieces are ready to go, arrange a mailing party to stuff, seal, stamp, and, if to be handwritten, address the envelopes. Never assign just one person to do all this hand work. Don't load everything that is to be mailed into a box and drop it off at a volunteer's house. That is a good way to lose a volunteer. Whether you have a mailing of 100 letters or 10,000, get everyone (including yourself) working on the project together to get the mailing out.

Make sure all your volunteers know what the letters say and see any supplemental materials that are being mailed with them. This lets everyone feel a part of the total effort and makes for more accurate word-of-mouth dispersal of information. Find a nice room with plenty of table space, provide refreshments, and make sure that your volunteers enjoy themselves. A sense of community and fun is part of the reason they give of their time.

If your mailing consists of less than 200 pieces, you will need postage stamps. The use of stamps has some advantages that may make them preferable in certain situations in spite of their higher cost. Stamped mail has a greater chance of getting a timely delivery. Stamps also add a personal touch and promote the same positive results as do hand-addressed envelopes.

Be careful when selecting stamps, however. Last year, I received a very well-written appeal from an antigun group that came in an envelope with a stamp picturing a well-known World War II general. The irony was interesting, but subliminally, it didn't help the appeal.

Keep track of the response to your mailing as you go along. Each time you receive a contribution, make up a *contributor card* for that person or organization. (Of course, if you're fortunate enough to have access to a computer, enter this information on that system.) Arrange these contributor cards in an alphabetical file and update them every time you receive a donation from this source, noting the date and amount of that contribution and through which fund-raising campaign or special event it was initiated. These cards provide an easy method of keeping annual totals on individual giving for program acknowledgments as well.

Sample Contributor Card

Name: A. H. McFee *Code:* BD
Address: 2820 E. 9th St., Kansas City, Mo.
Phone: 555-9842
Referred by: Don Brinker (board)

Date:	Drive:	Amount:
1/4/85	Luncheon	$ 50
2/6/86	Auction	$100
10/5/87	Rink Letter	$ 25

OCTOBER 15:

Follow-up phone calling begins.

This phase of the campaign involves one-to-one contact between a representative from your organization and a potential donor. Because this tactic requires a personal "out in the open" approach, it tends to bring up old bugaboos and fears about asking for money. It is extremely important that you set aside time and work very hard to overcome this potentially disastrous psychological block.

Hold individual or group training and motivational meetings during which you can take steps to help relax your volunteers. Anticipate their questions and concerns. Be very clear about what they are being asked to do and how they are to go about doing it. It is helpful to have a prepared script for your volunteer callers to use when they get on the phone. I would suggest something along these lines:

"Hello. I'm (name) and I'm calling on behalf of the Langford Action for Youth Committee project we wrote to you about. I wondered if you had any questions I could answer about our project. (Response.) I also want to invite you to the ice skating rink party we'll be having on the rink site at Broadway on Dodge on Saturday, November 24. We will be announcing the names of our contributors then and we hope we will be able to include you among them. I just want to remind you that our deadline for contributors is December 1 so that we can start using the rink this winter. Can we put you down for a donation? (Response.) Thanks very much. We'll look forward to seeing you on the twenty-fourth."

Obviously, the script is just a jumping off tool, serving to anchor the caller to the mission at hand. In the training meeting it is a good idea to set up a few role-playing exercises in which you play the potential donor being called and the volunteer assumes his or her role of telephone fund solicitor. This helps to alleviate tension and to develop different game plans to deal with the variety of attitudes and responses the volunteer will encounter over the phone.

Give each volunteer neatly typed up assignment/prospect cards with the name, phone number, and any pertinent data (i.e., "has eleven teenage sons" or "is a big supporter of Little League baseball") of each person to be called. Try to arrange each stack of cards to ensure positive reinforcement will occur. At a FEDAPT (Foundation for the Extension and Development of the American Professional Theater) conference I attended two years ago, a telethon consultant gave this advice: "Every time I give a volunteer a stack of prospect cards, I make sure at the top of that stack are at least five or six very strong prospects—people who might well give but also people who will be friendly, glad that your volunteer called them." Of course, if a volunteer knows a possible prospect, he or she should be the one to call that person.

The calls themselves should be to the point and will usually run no longer than three to five minutes with each volunteer making between ten and twelve an hour. Ideally, if the callers can work at the same time in the same space, it helps to create a "party" atmosphere, which goes a long way in reducing anxiety and increasing determination.

Don't allow your volunteers to feel abandoned. Don't just hand them their cards with a pat on the back and forget about them. Throughout this follow-up phase, keep reinforcing their activities on your organization's behalf. Check back with your volunteers periodically to see how they're doing. If people are having trouble with the phone calls, role-play the particular problem calls they have experienced. In an extended drive covering many thousands of prospects, you can keep up morale by distributing a simple newsletter or up-date report that lists the successes your volunteers are having and tells anecdotes from some of the more humorous calls.

Make sure you schedule a progress meeting before any follow-up calling begins. That way everyone has a goal to shoot for. If you are meeting on October 30 to see how you are doing, it gives a time frame for the calling and emphasizes a sense of personal responsibility to the effort.

OCTOBER 30

Hold a progress meeting to analyze how you are doing. (In a simple drive like this one, one or two of these meetings should be sufficient.) The meeting agenda should run something like this:

1. Call to order and introductions. Potential volunteers will show up throughout the course of your campaign, brought in by friends or inspired by the mailing or phone calls they

receive. Welcome them with open arms! Invite them to the progress meeting and make them a part of things.

2. Distribute and go over progress report. Have printed copies available for everyone at the meeting and mail copies of the report to absentees.

Sample Progress Report for Direct-mail Campaign

Progress Report No. ______
Date ____________

\# pieces mailed # People called
Yes No Maybe
Total Brought in ____ (% of total need: ____)

If the same drive is repeated from year to year, include comparison figures with last year's drive at this same point.

3. Analyze results/reassess goal. If results thus far are good, you can be pretty confident that you have chosen a goal that you will be able to accomplish. In that case, you can move on to the next step.

If, on the other hand, the campaign is doing poorly, hold a discussion on what needs to be changed. Would a postcard reminder be effective now? Door-to-door visits? A separate mailing to a different group of people in town? Or is your goal simply unrealistic for your group at this time? Don't be afraid to reassess your goal for the mail drive and adjust your plans accordingly. It is better to change your goal in mid-drive than to wait, hoping for a miracle, until the end and fall far short with no backup at the ready. If everyone seems to be doing his job well, but the mail drive still isn't working out, don't spend a great deal of time trying to analyze why. That you can do later, after the money is raised. Instead, spend your time coming up with new ideas to raise the funds. (See Chapter 6 on Troubleshooting.)

4. Develop a plan of action for the next two weeks. Assign

tasks for each volunteer to complete in this time period including:

a. Send out another press release to the media updating them on the progress of the drive (assuming, of course, that it is positive). Again, include your address so people can send you gifts after hearing or reading this announcement.

b. Complete follow-up calls.

c. Follow up on any pledges (people who said they would give) that haven't come in yet. Explain why the drive has to be completed by the end of November. (Winter is coming. . . .)

5. Schedule next progress meeting for the end of these two weeks.

AN IMPORTANT NOTE: Make sure you have something new to discuss or a positive report at each progress meeting. There is nothing worse than a series of negative "Oh, my God, we're in big trouble" meetings. Focus on the positive—what you can do (and there's *always* something that can be done) to turn things around.

NOVEMBER 1:

Hold a planning meeting for the ice skating rink party.

1. Go over the latest progress report and determine how much money still needs to be raised. That will be your goal for the rink party. If all that is still needed is $1,000, you can plan the low-key hot chocolate and doughnut morning where 200 people each give a $5 donation. If less than that is needed, it can be a true celebration party where you pass the hat for a related expense (such as putting in a soft drink machine). If more than that is needed, then emergency planning should take place to see if it is feasible to have the rink party be a bigger fund-raising event. (This is where corporate sponsorship or underwriting comes into play. How to get this type of support is discussed later in the chapter.)

2. Assign pre-party tasks (described in Chapter 6).

MID-NOVEMBER:

Progress meeting on party planning.

Go over details of arrangements for party, making sure everything is being taken care of. Assign day of event duties.

END OF NOVEMBER:

1. Hold the on-site rink party on November 24.
2. Announce to the press the success of the drive and the date construction on the rink will begin.

If all this sounds fairly matter-of-fact to accomplish, it is. Basically, the real key to successful fund-raising is planning—taking the time to lay out on paper what your goals are and the methods you will use to achieve those goals. Using volunteers is another key to a successful drive. Make them feel part of the goals and methods that you have decided to use. The more people who can call this cause—this campaign—their own, the better for all. Also note the importance that has been placed on the media. Using the media to get people excited about your plans goes a long way toward getting them to reach into their pockets to support you. Through your letters to individuals, in your phone follow-ups, with your various press releases and public service announcements, make sure you get out the good news. Fund-raising hasn't been done behind closed doors (realistically or metaphorically speaking) for years, and that is definitely not the way to do "Show Me" fund-raising. Open those doors and make it look inviting for people to come in.

There is one more step in your planning process that a surprising number of nonprofit organizations seem to forget: the wrap-up meeting. When the dust has settled, sometime within a week of the event, call all your volunteers together for a partylike meeting to hash over what went on and to thank them for their work. The input provided by your volunteers is important for tying up loose ends and gives you invaluable information to use in planning your next fund-raising project. A small gift or memento of the event or even a sincere letter of thanks will be appreciated. Remember, you'll need these people again, and you want to "Show Them" how much you value their time and services.

Door-to-door Drives

For a project that demands community involvement, such as the twenty-four-hour suicide hot line, direct one-on-one contact with people in the community is always preferable. Door-to-door campaigns can be huge and sophisticated operations like those organized by national political parties or they can be just as effective on a much smaller scale and very straightforward and simple in design. Again, the key is planning, asking the right questions to make sure the groundwork is solid.

1. *Financial Goal:* How much money do you need to bring in door-to-door? What will the average gift be? How many contacts will you have to make to achieve your goal?

Much as you set a goal for your overall need and develop a shopping list based on your projections of how to meet that goal, you need to pick a target number and devise a realistic plan to meet that number, given what you and your committee know about the members of your community (i.e., 200 door-to-door calls should yield 25 percent positive results of an average of $25 per call, resulting in a total of $1,250).

2. *Personnel:* Who will make these calls? As representatives of your cause and your organization, your canvassers must be knowledgeable in every aspect of your project and they must be comfortable about asking for money to support it. If they are all volunteers who have never fund-raised before, you must train them with role-playing exercises such as those described for phone call solicitation.

3. *Ammunition:* Besides their training, with what "Show Me" tools can you arm your canvassers? A flyer describing

your program is essential. A pen to fill out a check or pledge card is a good idea. A rubber stamp to put your group's name right on the check is another useful item. A gift for those who pledge or give is an excellent incentive. This is where you issue the invitation to the free concert and describe the graduated ticket/contribution system. The canvasser should have the concert tickets and gifts with him to present to supporters on the spot.

4. *Motivation:* How do you keep the volunteers working and working with enthusiasm? Schedule meetings to go over people's results, talk about problems, set new goals, hand out new prospect lists, and so on. Remember that door-to-door fund-raising work is difficult and can be wearing. Support and encouragement along the way is especially important.

5. *Record Keeping:* Make sure you keep good prospect or (if they give) contributor cards for each person contacted. Note whether they should be approached at a later date for money or if they are potential volunteers (another offshoot of door-to-door campaigning).

In spite of what may seem like a long process and a rather tedious way of raising money, the benefits of door-to-door campaigning are many. Once contact has been made door-to-door, chances are good that you have a very solid supporter, someone who will continue to support you in the future.

"Free" Concerts

By way of definition, we are using the word "free" to describe the concert, which costs your organization nothing (or very little) to put on in support of the twenty-four-hour hot line. It is "free" for people who have already given a goodly figure in the door-to-door campaign, but it is not free for anyone else. Indeed, it is a fund-raiser with a specific financial goal, just like the door-to-door campaign was.

How do you set up a free concert? Keeping in mind what type of music is popular in your community, make a wish list of groups that draw well and start inviting them to perform from the top of the list. A surprising number of musical acts will try out new material, preview a major tour, or simply put on a concert performance for charity if approached early enough. Willie Nelson, the Oak Ridge Boys, Dolly Parton, and Alabama are just a few examples of musicians in the country and western field alone who are famous for donating their services to help a nonprofit idea reach its financial goals.

We will discuss corporate sponsorship in depth later in this chapter, but for now, let me just insert it as an integral part of this type of fund-raising event. Start thinking early about which company or companies in your area should be approached to cover P.R., space rental, security, insurance, and other costs. Whether it is your local high school band or Johnny Cash, you'll find many businesses eager to lend their names to your activities because of the goodwill and publicity it garners for them.

Use the concert itself to help promote your cause. Make sure that at some point during the concert someone from your group—or, better yet, one of the performers—speaks on behalf of your project. Announce how much has been raised and how much still remains to be raised. Consider circulating among the audience anything from the proverbial hat for donations to pledge cards and pens. You have a captive audience of people who are enjoying themselves. Use this opportunity to get them behind your efforts.

Corporate Sponsorships

An important rule in Broadway theater producing is: "Never spend any of your own money." Let the same be said about fund-raising. A major tenet of the "Show Me" philosophy is that no organization should have to cover all the costs of a fund-raising project by itself. If at all possible, get sponsorship from local businesses or corporations, whether it be a simple mail campaign or an elaborate party. There's really a great deal of corporate money out there for the asking—it's *how* you ask that will make the difference between your organization and all the other nonprofits vying for these funds.

* * *

Smirnoff vodka ads picture violinist Pinchas Zukerman. Bankers Trust ads feature a scene from the ballet *Swan Lake.* A young artist stands atop a stool painting the first stroke on a huge canvas in MicroPro International's ad introducing its new word processor.

Why have these widely diverse types of companies chosen an "arty" image to advertise their products?

According to George Fasel, Vice-President, Corporate Communications, of New York City's Bankers Trust Company, "This recent use of the arts in advertising reflects an increased awareness by businesses that art is universally and immediately identifiable with excellence—a quality that corporate America wants associated with its products and services."

This same philosophy carries over from corporate advertising to corporate marketing and community relations programs. In Tucson, Arizona, the newly built Radisson Suite Hotel (a division of the Radisson Hotel Corp.) demonstrated its commitment to its new community by pledging to underwrite a fund-raising event for a different Tucson arts organization every year. Other local businesses jumped in to underwrite other costs for the first event, providing all kinds of food and drink, fashion shows, entertainment, mementos, and photography.

Mobil Oil, AT&T, and Exxon are just a few large corporations underwriting Public Broadcasting programs on television. Merrill Lynch has created a "Great Performances

Series" with twenty-five symphony orchestras across the country and is the sole corporate sponsor of the Metropolitan Opera's "Spring Tour." Philip Morris has donated the ground floor in its New York City headquarters building to be used as an art gallery, housing a branch of the Whitney Museum of American Art.

Corporate sponsorship of nonprofits is by no means limited to the arts. Both Scott Paper and Kimberly-Clark have introduced programs through which a portion of each sale of specific products will go to benefit a charitable organization. (Scott contributes to six voluntary health agencies, while Kimberly-Clark contributes to children's hospitals.)

Beer companies underwrite alcohol abuse programs. IBM donates computers to high schools. Softball manufacturers donate balls and bats to Little League teams. Local car dealers donate cars to driver's ed programs. Companies with in-house copying facilities print scripts for writers. The list of examples of corporate sponsorships could go on forever, and the nonprofit recipients of this support and the methods in which it is doled out are equally numerous. The motivation behind this outpouring of corporate generosity comes directly out of the "Show Me" philosophy. In addition to the tax breaks, the donating companies receive widespread publicity (when you list them in your program, ads, stationery, and so on) and a tremendous boost to their public image ("Exxon presents . . .").

Very often, a company that will not (or cannot) make a large money contribution to a nonprofit organization will agree to some sort of tie-in with that organization, donating goods, services, or a smaller amount of money. A donation of $5,000 cash may receive a small mention in the daily paper, but giving $5,000 to underwrite the costs of a celebrity gala or art auction or other type of visible fund-raiser will generate much more publicity in the media and with everyone attending the event.

In launching a fund-raising drive, any business—of almost any size—can be of benefit to you. Whether it will underwrite your total project costs or simply allow you late-night use of its memory typewriters, it is an invaluable resource. Remember, actual dollars are not the only things you need. Help in folding, stuffing, and mailing out your pieces is just as valuable as the dollar amount and staff time these efforts would take. Everything from free printing by banks to donated perfumes by cosmetic companies is out there for the asking.

One of the most important rules to remember is: *Find out whom you know.* Everybody—from the bank president sitting on your board to the sixteen-year-old volunteer envelope stuffer—knows somebody who can help you to foot the bill. How do you go about finding these tappable resources?

Developing a Corporate Shopping List

1. Have each member of your board, staff, and volunteer pool make a list of any close friends and/or family members that work for a corporation.
2. Make a list of places you do business with (personally and professionally). Everyone in our world can list at least twenty-five such businesses.
3. Keep a running list of corporations that have shown an interest in a cause or activity similar to yours. (Where have they given money before? Which ones have funded organizations similar to yours? Which have expressed an interest in the type of work your organization does?) Answers to these questions can be found through researching the standard library fund-raising references and through an ongoing study of the media.

Your best bets will be local sources. Work within the parameters of your area. If fast-food restaurants and mom-and-pop stores are the main businesses in your community, it's probably a waste of time to seek $10,000 in corporate underwriting. Remember the value of in-kind contributions of goods and services. Try to be as creative as possible when approaching local businesses so that you can help them fulfill your needs in a manner that is consistent with their business practices and financial realities.

If you live in a rural area that doesn't have many companies interested in giving to nonprofit groups and if your volunteers can't come up with any suggestions, in short if you don't have much of a corporate shopping list, try listening to the radio for a few nights. Tune to your public radio station to find out who is sponsoring their programming. Chances are good that any of the ten to thirty companies listed on a given night will be approachable by your group as well.

Corporate directories are another important source of valuable information. The three listed below profile the nation's top corporations and include such information as contacts' names and phone numbers, giving policy statements, geographical funding areas, and the type of giving they have done in the past. These directories keep their information updated and can be a good jumping off point for the solicitation of corporate underwriting, as well as grants.

The Corporate 500: The Directory of Corporate Philanthropy
Public Management Institute
358 Brannan Street
San Francisco, California 94107

The Corporate Fund-raising Directory
Public Service Materials Center
111 North Central Avenue
Hartsdale, New York 10530

The Corporate 1,000: A Directory of Who Runs the Top 1,000 U.S. Corps.
The Washington Monitor, Inc.
1301 Pennsylvania Avenue, N.W., Suite 1000
Washington, D.C. 20004

* * *

When actually approaching a business, having a personal contact—firsthand, secondhand, or even thirdhand—is invaluable. And it doesn't matter who actually makes the pitch—the person with the contact or you (or another member of your organization). The really important thing is to get that door opened. If the person with the contact will write or call his contact or allow you to use his name in your initial approach, the door is opened and positive results will much more likely follow. This is the easiest and best possible way to approach a business for support. May everyone who has to raise money have at least a few meetings set up this way in his or her career.

If your uncle doesn't happen to work for IBM (or whatever corporation or business that could help you out), do not despair. Remember, you've got something to offer them as well for the support you are seeking to get. The approach to a potential corporate sponsor is at once the most interesting, the most challenging, and the most frustrating part of this entire art form known as fund-raising. Let's look at the most difficult case possible.

Using the twenty-four-hour telephone hot line for suicidal teenagers as the project, let's say you want to get corporate underwriting to cover the $5,100 of fund-raising expenses budgeted to raise the support for the first year of the program. An obvious sponsor would be the local phone company—if not for money, then for free services or complimentary ad space in the Yellow Pages. But let's say you've seen in the newspapers that the PDQ Company has exhibited interest in helping the youth of your community. You've read that this company gives out four or five gifts a year that are between $5,000 and $10,000 in size. Their offices are in your community, but no one involved with your drive has any personal or professional contact with any of their employees. What to do?

Pick up the phone.

A general and widespread misperception seems to be that the corporate executive is sheltered by layer upon layer of individuals whose job it is to ward off random callers. Nowadays, however, most companies of even modest means have one or more people whose responsibility it is to take calls from prospective recipients of grants or other corporate gifts. These individuals might have several other responsibilities within the company as well (often they are in charge of human relations, public relations, community relations, special projects, and so on), but they also are supposed to work with the nonprofit groups that are interested in support from their company.

To quote Mrs. Alfred Lippmann, an active volunteer fundraiser for several organizations in New York City; "In sixty years of calling companies, I've found it is easier to get through to the 'right person' now than it was even ten years ago."

Thus, you are very likely to be able to speak to PDQ's head of corporate contributions on the telephone. When you do, or even if you simply get his or her assistant, try to set up a meeting to talk further about your needs. Avoid describing the project on the phone in too much detail. Keep that person interested enough so that he or she will want to talk to you. Here's an example of a model conversation:

"Hello. May I speak with the person responsible for corporate contributions from your company?"

"That would be Ms. Johnson."

"Is Ms. Johnson in?"

"I'll ring her office and see. . . ."

"Ms. Johnson? Hello. My name is ——."

"Yes. And what can I do for you?"

"I work with a volunteer group that wants to do something about teenage suicides in this city."

"Go on. . . ."

"Would it be possible to make an appointment to come in and see you?"

"Can't you tell me a bit more right now?"

"Our idea is a large one, and all we need is corporate support to help us raise the funds ourselves."

"I see."

"I could explain our idea in about twenty minutes if you'd be able to meet with me next week."

"Well."

"Any time that's convenient for you, of course. . . ."

"Well, if you put it that way. How about next Tuesday at eleven?"

"I'll be there. Thank you."

"Thank you."

The worst thing that can happen to you is that you'll never get through to the right person. If that happens, go for the second-best approach: Ask that the guidelines describing how PDQ Company gives money be mailed to you. Below is an actual set of contribution guidelines from NBC. We've reprinted them here, as they are representative of the type of corporate information most usually provided and requested by private funding sources.

Along with the company's guidelines, you'll also usually get a copy of the company's annual report, which will list at least some of their past corporate gifts. Many companies will also include some sort of application form to fill out. All of these materials will aid you in developing a personalized approach.

Whether your proposal is done on a corporate form or in

NBC CORPORATE CONTRIBUTIONS GUIDELINES—1988

The National Broadcasting Company, Inc. is proud to support non-profit organizations whose efforts reflect NBC's corporate goals and activities. NBC corporate support is generally dedicated to non-profit performing arts groups and broadcasting-related organizations. Special consideration is given to organizations which seek to develop new talent and audiences, especially for the theatre and film, and to organizations which serve constituencies nationwide. Grants may be provided for general operating expenses or for special projects.

NBC does not provide grants to NBC employees, other individuals, or religious groups; in addition, assistance is not customarily provided for capital campaigns or endowments.

Although NBC does not have a formal grant application form, requests for funding must be made in writing and must include the following:

1) A description of the organization, including its legal name, its primary purpose and history, and its chief distinguishing characteristics;
2) The grant amount requested;
3) A clear statement of the purpose for which the grant will be used, including a description of the benefits it is expected to provide; if support for a specific project is requested, a project budget must be included as well; if support was provided in 1987, explain how these funds were used;
4) An explanation of why you consider NBC to be an appropriate contributor to the organization;
5) Financial information, such as the organization's most recent annual report or an audited financial statement which documents current support/revenue and expenses;
6) Documents affirming that the organization is exempt from federal income tax under Section 501(c)(3) of the Internal Revenue Code, and a copy of the organization's most recent IRS Form 990;

Applications for funding in 1988 should be received no later than *August 7, 1987*. Please send your application, along with your completed Corporate Contributions Survey, to: Diane Osen, Manager of Community Services, The National Broadcasting Company, Inc., 30 Rockefeller Plaza, New York, New York 10112

NBC CORPORATE CONTRIBUTIONS SURVEY—1987

Please type and submit with grant application.

NAME/ADDRESS/TELEPHONE
____
____
____

KEY PERSONNEL/TITLES
____
____
____

MISSION STATEMENT
____
____
____

LOCAL/REGIONAL GROUPS SERVED
____
____

NEW TALENT/AUDIENCE DEVELOPMENT PROGRAMS
____
____

ANNUAL INCOME
Amount/percent earned: ______________
Amount/percent unearned: ______________

PREVIOUS NBC SUPPORT
Yes: __________ When (since 1980) ______
No: __________

501(C)(3) STATUS
Yes: __________
No: __________
Other: ______________

BENEFITS/DISCOUNTS
FOR NBC EMPLOYEES
Tickets: ______________
Membership: ______________
Other: ______________

a letter of proposal, it needs to contain the same seven pieces of information that we described earlier for direct-mail letters. To reiterate:

Key Elements of a Successful Fund-raising Letter:

- Describe the sender.
- Describe the reader.
- Establish the need for help.
- Pinpoint that need (your goal).
- State the project budget.
- Lay out the timeline for the drive.
- Describe how effectiveness of the drive will be measured.

Try to analyze each potential corporate donor's particular needs, interests, and desires—just as you would for an individual person from whom you were seeking aid. And then keep these needs, interests, and desires uppermost in your mind as you compose your letter seeking funds and services for your project.

Just as with a phone call, try to evoke interest about your project in a letter and try to schedule a face-to-face meeting, rather than set the stage for a fast yes or no answer. In-person meetings are also essential in securing in-kind contributions, which almost never can be worked out over the phone or through the mail.

If you are successful in setting up a meeting, you need to plan for that meeting in just as much detail as you'll be planning all other aspects of your fund-raising work.

If you have not had many meetings with people who are in the "business" of giving out money, then perhaps you should try some role-playing, which can allay your anxieties before going to a meeting to "pitch" your idea face-to-face. If possible, ask someone who works for another company or foundation to practice with you. Make sure that you are explaining your idea clearly and that you are not being timid about expressing what it is you need: $5,100 to cover the cost of a fund-raising drive to keep the hot line open and functioning for a year.

Also, collect any publicity or other printed materials you have that will enhance your credibility, underscore the problem you are trying to help solve, and stress the feasibility of your proposed solution to it. Prepare these materials in an easy-to-read manner. (A simple three-ring binder, neatly put together and well organized, can be very effective. Remember, you don't have to spend a lot of money to try to impress someone. Clarity and order go a long way in conveying professionalism.)

When the meeting time arrives, follow the general rules of good business practice. Arrive early, but not so early that it seems as if you are camping out in the PDQ offices. Dress conservatively but comfortably. You have twenty minutes to present not only your idea but yourself. Try to relax and be ready to discuss not only your project but other ideas and concerns Ms. Johnson (or whoever) might have. Think of yourself as PDQ Company's window on the world. Their corporate concerns are shared with your organization's concerns. This meeting should be an opportunity for the two of you to talk about these mutual concerns and one possible solution for them—your twenty-four-hour hot line.

If the meeting goes well, you'll be encouraged to submit a written proposal (a detailed version of the letter of proposal outlined earlier, including any specific information requested in your meeting). These days, most larger companies have a committee that meets weekly or monthly to review these proposals.

To speed the process, you can call back after, say, six weeks. Tell them about your other fund-raising plans—direct-mail campaign, special event, whatever you have scheduled—and that you would like to mention their support if it is, indeed, forthcoming—in the letters or publicity or program. Since this mention is great publicity, they just might speed up their decision-making process.

In any case, while you are waiting to hear from PDQ, develop a backup plan in case of rejection. Make up a second list of prospects to approach and follow through the same process with them if necessary. Use this time also to begin planning the other parts (i.e., direct mail, special event) of your funding campaign.

In addition to getting costs directly underwritten with funds, you can greatly reduce your fund-raising expenditures by getting in-kind donations of goods and services. Remember, your goal is to get all of your fund-raising expenses paid for by somebody else, so that you can put *all* the funds you raise into your project or program.

Ask companies, local businesses, and individuals to donate whatever goods or services you do not have underwritten. Again, the "Show Me" principles provide the drawing power. Having their name printed in your program is great publicity, and they will receive a tax deduction for the actual cost of the donated goods or services. With this to offer, you should be able to obtain free or low-cost food, liquor, flowers, table favors, photography, printing, and so on. Companies that are new in town or have a new product line coming out are especially eager to get public exposure and can greatly benefit from the word-of-mouth advertising they get by participating in your event. It's also good for their public image in the community. In the words of Don Reck, external programs manager for IBM in Arizona, "If you move to a new community, you just don't take what it has to offer. You have to give something back to make it better. It's not enough to merely be there. You've got to be involved and care." And companies want this involvement to be noticed.

I know of a small nonprofit group that hosted a cocktail party fund-raiser in which their only expense was for plastic cups and paper napkins. They approached a half-dozen caterers (who all wanted to be asked to bid on the group's and the guests' events in the future, of course) and asked them each to donate a quantity of just one hors d'oeuvre. They also approached a liquor dealer who had a new wine coming out on the market. The party was a huge success. Wanting to show themselves in their best lights, the caterers came through with their special delicacies, the wine flowed freely, and the guests loved having the chance to sample the interesting variety of cuisine. And it only took a few phone calls. (If they had read this book, they could have gotten the plastic cups and paper napkins donated as well.)

A group of food brokers supply charitable events with everything from salads to candy, free of charge. These wholesale merchants have set up a network that tells them when stores and restaurants are overstocked with various food items. The service, called Luncheon Is Served, will deliver these items to deserving fund-raising events in twenty-eight states. In their forty years of operation the group has helped raise over $35 million. The toll-free number to call is 1-800-421-0263.

Before putting your fund-raising budgetary expenses in ink, make sure you haven't left any stones unturned. Someone out there wants things you can offer. Show him what you can do to help him help you!

A WORD OF CAUTION: As much as we believe in the viability and accessibility of seeking corporate underwriting for nonprofit projects and fund-raising efforts, we urge you not to become overly dependent upon this or any one support resource. The disastrous position in which some nonprofits found themselves in the seventies resulted from an overdependency on government resources, and the same unfortunate pattern could recur with an overdependence on corporate resources.

In June 1986 Exxon announced that, due to the decline in the oil industry, it was forced to significantly reduce its contributions to the "Great Performances" public television series, and other oil companies predicted similar cutbacks in their underwriting efforts as well.

James P. Roscow, a business writer and historian, suggested a diversified solicitation of corporate sources in the May 1986 issue of *Natural History* magazine.

> The array of private and public dollar support seems substantial today and apt to be more so tomorrow. But the future presents a challenge. One element is the volatility of corporate earnings. . . . The challenge for not-for-profit organizations is to identify new business segments without a strong contributions history (technology, health, and recreation industries) and discuss contributions with them.

In addition, as we've stated before, never put all your eggs in one basket. Don't depend solely on the government or corporations or foundations or individual contributions. The "broad base of support" theory means a combination of a variety of these sources with backup plans built in to ward off disaster.

And now, let's explore the various types of "disasters" we could encounter and how to avoid them. . . .

Resource List: Chapter 4

If you want to start a library about the subject of planning and research, here you go:

Monthly Letter

American Association for Corporate Contributions
P.O. Box 6401
Evanston, Illinois 60204

Pittsburgh Media Guide
The Community Technical Assistance Center
307 Fourth Avenue, Suite 1305
Pittsburgh, Pennsylvania 15222

Catalog of Mailing Lists
Alvin B. Zeller (one of many firms that sell lists)
37 East 28
New York, New York 10016

Telepledge: The Complete Guide to Mail-Phone Fund-raising
by Louis A. Schultz
The Taft Group
5130 MacArthur Boulevard
Washington, D.C. 20016

chapter 5

SPECIAL EVENTS

> Giving people what they want may be the most overlooked aspect of special events. Happy guests and sponsors have a tendency to be generous when the charity comes calling again.
>
> —The Southall Group

As grant proposals were to traditional fund-raising, special events are to the new "Show Me" fund-raising. From rock star concerts for tens of thousands to cocktail parties for ten loyal subscribers, special events are a great way to give supporters something for their dollar. Holding special events requires a different kind of preparation and action from other types of fund-raising, since they involve in-person, on-site orchestration of both the event and the people attending. In this chapter we will walk through a special event luncheon, based on the model of the senior tour fund-raising luncheon, but bear in mind that the same type of planning and follow-up is applicable, with adjustments, to any type or size of special event.

Nuts-and-bolts Planning

Finally "the" day dawns. Before the well-earned back-patting and sighs of relief can take place, the "on-site" work must be accomplished. If you have a well-thought-out game plan, this "work" can be so enjoyable that you may feel sorry when it's over. Important tasks, such as developing a good relationship with your guests and getting everyone to have a good time while giving them a sense of being part of a special mission, need not be fraught with tension. Worry-free techniques exist that allow you to handle last-minute details. Make sure you delineate and divide up duties among staff and volunteers and make certain you'll be equipped for every situation (expected and unexpected). In other words, you can—and must—be in control of the situation, rather than the other way around.

We've already mentioned several kinds of special events, so you are probably bursting with ideas for your own special event fund-raiser—if one seems appropriate for your group. (Sometimes people catch "special event fever" and try to carry one out no matter what. Watch out for this epidemic—a special event can be premature or, depending upon your resources, too costly to pull off correctly; another type of fund-raising effort may be much more practical and productive at this point.)

But now we've done our analysis and decided to hold a luncheon as the final step in this particular project, which is to send a group of senior citizens to Washington, D.C., to bring greater attention to their problems. Let's go through the step-by-step process for this luncheon—a process that can be the basis of almost any special event—an auction, a barbecue, a concert—you may undertake. We begin with questions that will lead to a direct plan of action:

1. What is our goal?

You've raised all but $2,000 for the seniors' trip to Washington, D.C., so that's what you need to bring in at the luncheon. The seniors themselves and other volunteers can set up and serve, and you probably can get a local restaurant or group of restaurants to donate the food and perhaps the space for this luncheon. Or if you're in one of twenty-eight states where the organization (described in Chapter 4) operates, use their services.

If you charge $20 a ticket, with your overhead charges virtually eliminated by donated services, you'll reach the goal by selling only 100 seats.

If you are unable to get your food (or other) costs covered (and let me recommend you do everything possible to get them covered—it's much easier that way!), you'll need to make adjustments. Either raise the individual ticket price or sell more tickets.

Another consideration in selecting a ticket price is, of course, your audience. If $20 is too steep in your area, then think about 200 tickets at $10 each. It's far easier to go after greater numbers of people than to try to get an unrealistic amount of money out of a smaller number. (For some projects, when media attention is the goal, a low ticket price may be desirable to ensure a packed crowd.)

Have a committee of people organized to make sure that tickets are sold. The personal touch is essential here. A note on the invitation or an in-person visit or phone call really makes a difference. Even a "Do sit at my table," signed by a friend, goes a long way when selling special event tickets.

NOTE: I always refer to tickets *sold*. An overabundance of complimentary tickets to a special event is the most common hinderance to a financial goal being met. Be strict right from the start about who will be comped and who won't. (A guideline I've always used is that for tickets under $50, no one should be comped.) You may decide to comp a local politician, minister, TV personality, committee members, and so on, but you'd be surprised how many guests of honor or committee members will be glad to pay, especially if their payment is acknowledged in the introductory speech or program copy: "Mr. Smith believes in what we are doing so much that he not only agreed to come here and speak today—he turned down our offer of a complimentary ticket and insisted on paying!"

2. What will the program be?

This question should be answered long before the event. As mentioned earlier, it's easier to write an effective invitation when you include details of the actual program in it. Last-minute changes can always be made to accommodate the celebrity who just happens to be in town, but work out the details of who will be doing what well ahead of time.

Keep your structured program short! Twenty to thirty minutes at a luncheon is more than sufficient. A luncheon that drags on forever does more harm than good for your cause and puts a definite damper on repeat business. Here is a suggested program for the seniors' tour luncheon:

> *12:00:* Check-in and before-luncheon cocktails. (These days, fewer and fewer people drink hard liquor, so it is perfectly acceptable—and, of course, cost-saving to have a cash bar for those who want it and to serve only white wine and soft drinks as the free-of-charge beverages. Again, local liquor distributors are very approachable for donations of a case or two of wine in return for a plug during your event.)
>
> *12:20:* Seating. (Any sit-down meal for under 300 people should have individual place cards at each table and printed table list guides distributed at check-in. For groups over 300, place cards can be eliminated, but table lists for seating should still be used. Designated seating makes everything flow much more smoothly and—by placing a board member or celebrity, staff/volunteer/target group member among guests—can also be used as a fund-raising tool.
>
> *12:30:* Appetizer or salad or soup should be at everyone's place so they can begin eating while introductions are made at the podium. Introductions should concentrate on the reasons why everyone has come to the event—

to help reach a goal. If grace is to be said, call on a clergyman at this time.

12:40: Main course is served. Allow people to eat and talk with each other uninterrupted by any formal program.

1:10: Coffee and dessert are served. Again, you or another member of your group speak of the reasons for the drive and the luncheon. A short history lesson of the problems or needs being addressed and progress thus far would be appropriate here. Reading letters (or, for better dramatic effect, telegrams!) in support of your cause helps to set the tone for the rest of the luncheon.

1:15: Introduce guest of honor/main speaker. For the seniors' tour this could be anyone from a local celebrity in the senior citizen age group, the mayor of your town, or a congressman. This person's job is to give the meaty speech of the program, outlining the problem in dramatic terms and lending their support to your group's activities. Be sure this speaker is given a time limit—I'd say twenty minutes at most—and make sure he or she sticks to it. (Unless the person is running for reelection, most will welcome this limitation set by you.)

1:35: You make final remarks, including acknowledgments of financial and other help received, a thank-you to your guests, and an announcement and congratulations on meeting your $2,000 goal, enabling the group of seniors to go to Washington!

1:45: Your guests can be on their way. If a giveaway gift is to be handed out (and I would urge you to provide one), this is the time to do it. (Every cigarette manufacturer makes small giveaway packs they will contribute for free and usually even deliver and put out on the tables for you. If a local merchant allows you to give out their personalized matches, suddenly you have a table full of take-home items.) A small giveaway can be placed next to the table settings. As mentioned earlier, it should be possible to get a wide variety of gifts donated by manufacturers or local merchants, who will receive not only a goodwill mention in your program but a chance to increase their business through this sampling of their products among your guests.

Door prizes can also be obtained from local merchants to add to the excitement. For example, you can tell everyone that a gold star has been placed on the bottom of one of the plates, and as soon as they finish eating, they should turn their plate over.

This is as straightforward a luncheon schedule as possible, so that it can be adapted to suit almost any purpose. There can be many variations on this schedule, of course. You may want to include skits or music or film/slides. How your program is arranged will depend on the resources—celebrities, guest speakers, and other special people—available to you. You may want to serve buffet-style. The essential thing is to plan to the minute and adhere to that plan as closely as possible. Timing is one of the most important factors in the success of a special event.

And what of the mechanics? What must take place behind the scenes to make sure that everything goes off smoothly as planned?

3. Who does what?

Special events call for maximum use of volunteer help. Happily, they are also the easiest type of fund-raising method to enlist this volunteer help for. People who might feel shy about going door-to-door or calling on the phone will usually be enthusiastic about assisting a special event project. Even the smallest event has an aura of excitement to it and the teamwork approach takes away many individual anxieties.

Following is a list of the number of volunteers you will need and the duties that you will need them for. Note that most jobs can be doubled up if you don't have a lot of helpers. You can never have too many helpers, but if it looks like everyone on your guest list has been assigned a task, it's time to change your luncheon into a victory celebration!

The day before the event make up a *division of responsibilities* sheet delineating each job and the names of the people responsible for each. Photocopy, distribute, and go over the sheet with your group either the day before or the morning of the event, so that everyone is clear on what his or her duties are.

• *Setting up the tables* (3 to 10 people): Depending on the size of your guest list and the number of volunteers, your group should arrive one to two hours ahead of time at the event site. Assign each person or group specific items to put on the tables. A checklist of these items includes:

1. Place cards and table numbers. Work out place settings in advance, devising a floor plan of the room and individual table lists.

2. Programs, journals, pledge cards, and any other printed materials.

3. Small table favor items (giveaways).

• *Check-in:* A long table divided into alphabetical sections is the best setup for a smooth flow of traffic. The check-in table should look something like this:

Sample Check-in Table

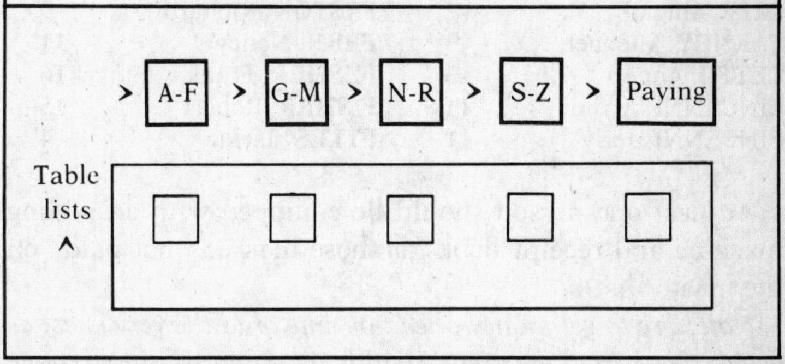

There is really no need to issue tickets—it only makes for extra printing and postage costs and headaches when people lose or forget them. Print up table seating lists, in alphabetical order as below, which can be used for check-in as well as to guide each person to his or her seat. As a person is checked in, give him or her a copy of this list. (These lists also allow people to locate friends or acquaintances at other tables and to see overall who is attending the event.)

Sample Seating List

Senior Sense 10th Anniversary Luncheon

Name	Table #	Name	Table #
-A-		-D-	
ADAMS, Carol	16	DEVEREAUX, Janice	12
ALCON, James	12	DEETS, Bernard	10
ANDERSON, Bud	7	DENBURG, Susan	3
ARLEN, June	11	DICKENSON, Steven	4
ASBURY, Quentin	7	DICKENSON, Margaret	10
		DYSEN, Linda	11
-B-			
BAKER, Mary	15	-E-	
BEESLEY, John	1	EBERSOL, Melanie	2
BERESFORD, Carolyn	12	EGGERTON, Joan	1
BEEKMAN, Tom	14		
		-F-	
-C-		FANTO, Gloria	10
CAPP, Abigail	2	FASTON, Richard	9
CARNEY, Michael	3	FERR, Nancy	11
CETTO, Anne	13	FESHER, Frank	16
CINCENNI, Arthur	11	FISHER, Robert	15
CINCENNI, Judy	11	FYLES, Jackie	4

At least one person should be equipped with an adding machine and receipt book for those marked "not paid" on the master list.

Note: Try to get money ahead of time or at the very latest as people check in at the event. It adds time and trouble to have to bill people after the event is over. And, sad but true, there will be a few who will attend and then not pay.

• *Guides* (2 to 3 people): After people receive their seating lists, have volunteers on hand to help them find their tables (especially important at a large event). People will also want to know the location of telephones, rest rooms, coatroom, dining room, and so on. Guides standing ready to answer these questions help eliminate bottlenecks at the entrance.

Designate at least one of these guides as floor captain. This person should act as troubleshooter. Equipped with a master list of seating arrangements, he or she should have the diplomatic skills necessary to handle last-minute problems or changes.

• *Runners* (1 to 3 people): Before, during, and after the event, there is often a great deal of message sending—people canceling, instructions from the head table to the kitchen, and so on. They can be handled easily if some volunteers are designated to deal with them.

• *Cleanup* (3 to 5 people): After the guests leave, there is still work to be done. Make sure there is a cleanup crew that will stay to pick up any leftover gifts or printed materials from the tables, check for purses or coats left behind, and just generally get the room back to the way you found it.

Thanking the head waiter and chef is a good idea, especially if you plan on coming back for another event. (If your event has been profitable, it's also wise to leave tips. Generally, if the meals were donated, tips should be based on their actual retail value.)

Media Coverage

In discussing the various fund-raising projects for our model programs—the ice skating rink, the hot line, and the seniors' trip to Washington, D.C.—we've included ways to incorporate public relations techniques into our planning so as to obtain coverage by the media. Nowhere is the opportunity to get extensive media coverage greater than in conjunction with a special event. Do whatever you can to get as much media coverage as possible. Think of the value of P.R. and coverage by the media as almost equal to the value of the dollars you want to pull in.

What can media coverage do for you?

• It can provide free advertising to promote your project, resulting in ticket sales and contributions of dollars, goods, and services.

• It can provide the lure and the reward of public recognition—one of the most valued "Show Me" gifts you can offer potential contributors in this media-conscious age.

• It can help you to be successful in your future fund-raising efforts by strengthening your credibility and increasing your arsenal of support materials.

• It can save a failing drive by giving you the necessary extra boost to reach your goal.

How do you get media coverage?

Obviously, the media will not cover everything you do. Decide which part of your fund-raising campaign has the most potential for coverage and focus the attention on it. (Is it the free concert? The victory dinner? The door-to-door campaign? What?)

1. Story ideas. Usually, you can expect to get two—or at most three—stories out of a drive. If it is newsworthy (and it is up to you or your publicity person to make it sound newsworthy), the first story is the *announcement* of your drive or event. (See pages 73–74 for *Sample Press Release.*) The second story is centered on the *culmination* of the drive or event (if your goal was met), reporting the results in as glowing and as exciting terms as possible. This can often be an expansion of the announcement made at the special event. Third is the *special,* perhaps quirky, slant on your activities that captures the interest and attention of the media (the mayor signing your direct-mail letter, a bake sale run by octogenarians, the first grant ever from a new corporation).

2. Follow through. Give at least one person in your organization the task of making sure that what you want covered is described to the media more than once. Just sending

out a press release will not do the job. Follow-up phone calls, adjunct materials (press kit, progress updates, unexpected incident reports), and assistance in physically getting the press to your event are key responsibilities of this person. Be sure this person is well informed about all aspects of the drive or event, your organization, and your goals, so that he or she can answer any questions and further promote your cause.

3. Treat your media people as you treat your potential contributors.

Media coverage can be just as important as dollars to the success of your efforts. Make sure the media understands how important they are to your success. (Also remember that almost all local newspapers, television, or radio affiliates do give support to nonprofit groups, both in-kind and in cash, as well as providing coverage.)

The media, just like potential contributors, should get invitations, phone calls, visits, all support materials, and so on. In other words, make them feel like they are a vital part of your event or drive.

4. Help the media to write or photograph or tape a good story. Be clear and concise about details of the drive. Highlight what you think are the most essential points in terms of your success. When writing a press release, put the most important information first. If it is a matter of getting the right person together with the reporter for an interview or dropping off photos or assigning a volunteer to assist the cameraman at the event itself, do it without hesitation. Even if you are sold out or your drive is completed, cooperate with the media in any way they request—there's always going to be a next time, and any kind of goodwill and personal contact you can build within the media will ultimately be to your very great advantage!

5. Show your appreciation. "Show Me" methodology is just as important a tool when dealing with the media as it

is when dealing with your contributors. If you're giving out perfume or a tie at your dinner, make sure you include the media. A letter of thanks, a personal phone call of appreciation, a memento of the event—whatever you do for the people who ran the cameras or wrote the article will be remembered.

Eleventh-hour Tricks

What if you are ostensibly holding a victory party but are still $2,000 shy of your goal? What if your drive is falling slightly below projections? You need a surge of adrenaline to get over the top. Following are three of the many ways to encourage the friends and supporters who have gotten you this far to make the leap, joining in a final push to the goal. Here's how to get additional monies at the event itself:

On-the-spot Pledges

Unique to a special event are the momentum and energy that can be used to your advantage for some extra fund-raising. You have 200 people gathered together in a room who are all supporters; a certain amount of money has already been raised; the cameras are on; the speeches have been made; the gifts will soon be given out—all of a sudden, someone from one of the head tables stands up and offers to pay $1 for every $5 that is pledged to help your cause make it to the goal. If pledge cards (see page 175) have been placed on each chair or are readily available to be distributed (with souvenir pens to be kept as mementos of the event), then you have the start of what should be impressive on-the-spot pledging. It is one of the oldest tricks in the fund-raising book, but it continues to work beautifully. Just make sure you have two or three people primed to start the pledges off. There is nothing more disastrous than to have the cameras (real or metaphorical) rolling but no one to kick off what should become a dramatic chain reaction.

NOTE: It is possible to get good results from on-the-spot pledging without having someone create a challenge situation as outlined. But there needs to be some sort of kickoff to get the ball rolling. It could be accomplished with the announcement of several large checks presented at the event itself or by creating a telethon-like atmosphere, counting down the last dollars needed to meet the goal.

Special Sponsorships

If you are still shy of your goal at a special event or even during the course of the fund drive, you may want to add to your various categories of supporters. Announce at the special event or at a specific point in the fund drive a category that suggests a gift that is above and beyond all the others, i.e., Producer, Ultimate Angel, Major Domo. Most veteran fund-raisers keep one or two of these special categories in their hats as a lure for the last-minute sizable gift. This technique works well with a corporation that steps in to cover all the costs of your event or can be used to encourage an individual to offer the kickoff challenge for on-the-spot pledging.

Additional Donors

The basic premise behind special event fund-raising is to create an atmosphere in which people are gathered together and enjoying themselves. What better time to add to your shopping list of potential givers? Your master of ceremonies can easily get everyone to write down the names and addresses of four or five friends and neighbors who can be approached after the event. Having these personalized lists helps your approach in wondrous ways. Here is an example of how it might work in a fund-raising letter to these new contacts:

Dear ______________:

As you might have heard from (name of person who suggested this potential donor) last night, the ABC project raised over $4,000 at a dinner party that will be talked about in our community for some time to come.

At this party your name was suggested as an individual who might like to help us raise the final $2,000 needed to reach our goal. Once we reach this goal, we will be able to (what you will be using money for).

Enclosed please find information that (again, the name of person who gave this name) thought you'd be interested in seeing.

Thank you for considering this request.

Sincerely,

NOTE: Any of these last-minute techniques can be helped immeasurably by media attendance. The media can make an event or drive come alive with excitement. There is nothing better for stimulating the flow of adrenaline so important to motivating potential donors than the presence of a television camera or two or even a reporter making good use of a notebook and pencil.

* * *

The key to all of the ideas described in this chapter is getting the maximum energy and enthusiasm for your project. Fund-raising is no longer a dry, silent practice that takes place in small offices far from the public eye. Fund-raising has become a true art form of the people—open to one and all.

"Remember when they used to send us poverty programs! . . ."

Doug Marlette
The Charlotte Observer
King Features Syndicate

Resource List: Chapter 5

To stress the importance of media coverage of special events, I list only two resources for further reading (both on media):

The Media Resource Guide: How to Tell Your Story
Edited by Chuck Rossie
ACA Books
570 Seventh Avenue, Department 24
New York, New York 10018

Pittsburgh Media Guide
The Community Technical Assistance Center
307 Fourth Avenue, Suite 1305
Pittsburgh, Pennsylvania 15222

chapter 6

TROUBLESHOOTING

"When I want to know what the trouble is around here, Metcalf, I'll hire a troubleshooter."

As everyone knows, even the best-thought-out plans worked out into the most minute details can go astray. This chapter is perhaps the most important in this book. Learning how to prevent mishaps is essential to succeed in your fund-raising efforts. Equally important is knowing what to do when things do go wrong. This pre-project troubleshooting is so vital to the success of *every* venture that we are devoting an entire chapter to the topic.

Special Events

First, let's examine three case histories of fund-raising events that got themselves into trouble. The first occurred over one hundred years ago in conjunction with a project we are still fund-raising for today—the Statue of Liberty. It points up the value of having strong business contacts associated with your organization. In this case, a businessman came through with a solution that transformed what looked like a clear-cut disaster into success:

Although they had been campaigning to raise funds for a decade, in March 1885 the American Committee for the Statue of Liberty had only $3,000 left from the $182,491.40 they had raised, and they needed $100,000 more to fund their project to provide a pedestal for the statue.

Joseph Pulitzer, publisher of *The New York World,* came to the committee's rescue. His newspaper launched a full-scale drive to his widespread readership. With pennies from children, single dollar bills from the elderly, and other small contributions, the goal was reached in only five months!

Obviously, the fact that this committee went through $179,000 before getting their project off the ground means they were doing something seriously wrong. Much more recently another organization found itself facing a similar problem.

Two years ago, a major New York charity scheduled the Waldorf for a fund-raiser with a million-dollar goal. Some of the most prominent people in New York were on the planning committee. They planned a winter theme and chose the month of January to avoid the holiday schedule but still stay far enough away from April 15 to avoid any large tax payment problems among the invitees. Invitations went out on time. The evening's program was organized well enough ahead of time so that a good mix of local celebrities and entertainers would appear preceding the dinner/dance. Arrangements were worked out with designers and florists to turn the Grand Ballroom into a winter wonderland.

All seemed to be going well until someone figured out that the cost of food, decorations, invitations, gifts, and so on (in short, the budget for the event) was going to exceed the $1 million they hoped to raise for the charity. Even if they sold $1 million worth of tickets, they could still quite easily lose money for the charity!

Luckily, this committee had monied contacts. The night before the event, a board member found an anonymous angel who underwrote the $1 million cost of throwing the ball. Literally saved at the eleventh hour, the event became an even greater success than anticipated.

This example and the next show that no matter how well staffed and well heeled the organization is that is throwing the fund-raiser, problems do occur.

Of course, planning is the best way to avoid problems. Whether raising a few thousand dollars for an ice skating rink or $1 million for a hospital, it is essential to cover the basics. A well-thought-out budget, plus efforts to obtain underwriting or in-kind donations of goods and services, probably would have forestalled the charity's money problems.

Having a major backer "in reserve" for the once or twice in your lifetime when you need extraordinary help such as described above is one sure solution to an overextended budget, but not the only one by any means. The overextended budget is really a universal dilemma. I guarantee you that anyone who has ever staged a special fund-raising event has sooner or later run into this problem. Those who have lived to put together another event have learned how to solve that problem.

An alternative solution to the wealthy backer for overspending is more difficult but essential. Build a cutoff figure into your budget. Make sure that everyone in your organization understands that if the expenses exceed this limit, you will cancel the event. The knowledge should motivate everyone to find ways to keep the costs down, but it is no idle threat. You must make money on a special event fund-raiser. No one benefits from a benefit that loses money.

Another recent fund-raiser suffered from what could be called an embarrassment of riches—not money riches (an impossible happenstance in fund-raising) but people riches. I think it's obvious that incorporating celebrities (whether they be from your local high school baseball team or Hollywood) in your fund-raising plans is a valuable "Show Me" draw. But is it possible to have too many? Let's take a look at an embarrassing national fund-raiser where this very situation occurred:

Alexander Cohen and his wife, Hildy Parks, are famous Broadway producers and entrepreneurs. They have lent their expertise to numerous charitable events and are especially noted for their annual Tony Award presentations on television. In 1985 they decided to stage a "Night of 100 Stars" at Radio City Music Hall to benefit the Actors' Home, a retirement facility for members of the actors' union. One hundred celebrities would lend their talents to a one-night gala variety show that also would be filmed for future television broadcast. It is hard to say no to a cause as worthy as the Actors' Home. Adding in the panache and polish of Alex and Hildy gives you an event certain to attract a good collection of celebrities. And that is exactly what happened.

The "100 Stars" became 380. With the stops and starts for television, the "night" turned into an interminable six-hour ordeal, as enough celebrities to make up three or four fund-raisers were squeezed uncomfortably into one. It became infamous as the one that people were glad they missed.

Don't think this can't happen to you. Inviting two politicians running for the same political office can automatically add an hour onto your program. Even rival religious figures have been known to get involved in one-upmanship, seeing who can pray the longest at a special event. How do you avoid this?

The key is to work out a program well ahead of time. Often the program is the last detail to be considered. The theory is that the tickets should be sold and the money raised before much time is spent on the actual evening's schedule. Wrong! Outlining your program is an integral part of the initial stages of planning the overall event. Timing can be as key to a successful outcome as filling the room. Again, if you want to be able to stage special events (and remember that a special event can be as small as a cocktail party for ten loyal supporters) on a regular basis, each and every one needs to be a success—both financially and socially.

Usually, a core of people in any community are the ones that attend fund-raising events on a regular basis. So you must consider those factors that will ensure repeat business. These regular attendees are busy people who will not tolerate unnecessarily long speeches or introductions. Make sure to plan your event as close to the minute as possible. Use only the number of celebrities you can comfortably fit into a reasonable program. Let each celebrity or speaker know the time frame at the outset so he or she can plan accordingly. This prevents misunderstandings or hard feelings.

A trick I use is to include the program as a part of the invitation itself. You always get a few complaints from people who feel they've been left out. ("I should be speaking because it was my newspaper article that first suggested the idea of a twenty-four-hour hot line!") But you'll get those anyway, and having them come well before the event, rather than during or after it, allows enough time to work them in.

This printed program can be part of the invitation or an insert. It doesn't have to be detailed, but it should be clear about starting and ending times.

Sample Invitation

Senior Supports
invites you to
The 10th Anniversary Senior Sense Luncheon
Tuesday, April 14, 1987
The Hotel Frances
125 Magnolia Street
Cocktail Reception 11:30 A.M. (Patio Room)
Luncheon served promptly 12:45 (Garden Restaurant)
Luncheon ends 2:00 P.M.
Speakers: Mayor Scott M. Carter
Janet Robertson
Dr. Joanne Storch
Music: The Old-Timers Band

In addition to the problems described in these examples, there are a number of other common horrors that have been known to beset special events. They include:

Poor Timing

In addition to the internal timing of the event program, be sure you do a clearance check on the actual date of the event itself (i.e., Super Bowl Sunday is not a good day to schedule a fund-raiser). Every community has a source (be it the newspaper, chamber of commerce, or, in larger cities, a special events network service) where you can find out what is scheduled on any given date. If the competition looks too threatening, no matter if it is the anniversary of the birth of the person around whom your event is organized, choose another day.

Our old friend Bob Geldof learned this lesson when he scheduled his Sport Aid (another campaign for African famine relief, involving races and other athletic events) at the same time as the Hands Across America event in recognition of American hunger. The project itself was definitely not the problem, as Sport Aid was a huge success in Europe, where it was the only game in town. In the United States, however, where it had to compete with the heavily publicized Hands Across America, Sport Aid attracted only thin crowds and just 4,000 runners took part in the New York City race.

Likewise, Willie Nelson's Farm Aid II lost out to the Statue of Liberty centennial celebration against which it was scheduled. Farm Aid I had brought in $9 million, but II's take was only up to $1.3 million by the end of the day of the event, and even with late contributions was expected to wind up far below the first event's total. According to concert spokeswoman Margaret Wade, the Fourth of July—"especially when it's the Statue of Liberty's birthday"—might not have been the best day for the show. "The people who could afford it probably watched the Statue of Liberty."

Inappropriate Setting or Activity

A moonlight hayride with a picnic dinner under the stars in a cow pasture may be your idea of a perfect romantic evening. Someone else who doesn't share your passion for the great outdoors might think of this same agenda as an exercise in discomfort. When planning your event, put yourself in your supporters' shoes.

Find out what they like to do and where they like to do it. A quick survey of audience members (which could be done at performances or like events or by phone) is not inappropriate. You can't please all the people all the time, but with a bit of audience research, you'll be able to attract and please a lot more of them.

Overselling

What happens if you oversell? ("How can this happen?" you ask. It is not as difficult as you might think. If your volunteer committee members each go over their goal and/or if word of mouth attracts more people to your event than you anticipated, it can and does happen.) You can, of course, give the money back and encourage these people to send their money in sooner next time, but you are not booking a Rolling Stones concert. You're trying to raise much-needed funds for your meaningful cause or program. Before sending that money back, look at some of your alternatives:

First of all, it is a well-known rule of fund-raising life that a certain small percentage of people who have paid to attend a special event will not attend. Hugh Weir, the Special Events Manager at the Plaza Hotel in New York City, estimates that between 3 and 8 percent of those who paid will not show. At a recent special event planning meeting, he said that in his experience Brooke Shields and Ronald Reagan are the only headliners who guarantee that every seat will be taken.

Thus, you can build in a "seating where we can" policy, in which latecomers are guaranteed a seat but they just won't know where that seat will be until moments before the event begins. If there are enough no-shows, your problem is solved by giving the latecomers these empty seats. If not, ask staff members or volunteers to agree to give up their seats if need be. Make up a list of these people beforehand so that the last-minute filling in can be conducted in a swift and orderly manner.

- Talk to the hotel or restaurant where your event is being

held. Don't be afraid to ask them to help you figure out a solution. Often, they can expand their rooms to include more people, and since they usually charge by the person, they too do better financially with the higher attendance.

• Think about holding your event twice. A small dance company in Atlanta recently held their first opening night gala. They only had room in the auditorium for 70 paid guests. Ten days before the event all 70 seats were already sold, and the orders continued to pour in. The dancers agreed to do one performance at seven o'clock and another at eleven, and the reception (which was held in an adjoining gallery, where up to 200 people could be accommodated) was scheduled in between the two shows. People coming for the seven o'clock show mingled with those coming for the eleven o'clock show, and two small groups combined to create a very festive and much more lucrative fund-raiser for the company.

• In planning your event, don't overlook the possibility of offering "special" tickets at double or even triple the price. If you may sell out, this is a great way to get extra money for the same amount of seats. Veteran special event planners claim that those "special" special event tickets usually sell out faster than the regularly priced ones because people want whatever this special status affords them. Be sure to provide that special return for their extra dollars with preferred seating, seating with celebrities, a special commemorative gift, or some other valued advantage.

Panic

Your tickets aren't sold. Your celebrity guest of honor has been indicted and can't make it. The hotel burned down with all of your decorations up. A snowstorm has paralyzed the city for two weeks. All of these are great excuses for panic. The word "panic" connotes fear, apprehension, disaster. It also connotes a huge amount of nervous energy, usually misdirected into the wrong action.

I'd like to suggest that panic is one of the least-used tools of successful fund-raising. I think you can learn to turn almost any problem situation to your advantage. Here are some examples of how to channel panic energy creatively and make it work for you:

Tickets Aren't Sold

This is the most common special events-related problem. Your invitations might have gone out late. Another event scheduled on the same day may be taking your supporters away. In any case, for whatever reason, your tickets simply are not selling. What to do?

First, make up a timetable in which you divide up the remaining tickets to be sold and map out goal dates to sell them by for each batch:

Sample Timetable

# Tickets to Sell	*Date Must Sell by*	*% of Total Sales Completed*
20	June 1	25%
20	June 15	50%
20	June 30	75%
20	July 15	100%

Get the press to help you sell tickets. Send out an update press release about plans for the event in which you focus *positively* on selling tickets. Sample tag lines to include would go along these lines:

- "100 tickets still left for dance."

- "Only 20 more couples will be able to attend ice skating rink party."
- "Seniors need to find 200 people to help them go to D.C."

Schedule an emergency meeting of your volunteer committee and go over individual sales. Talk through problems people are having. Decide whether you need to put additional measures into motion, such as sending out another mailing to a second group of people, conducting follow-up phone calls, sending out reminders, and so on.

Your Program Has Fallen Apart

Fund-raising history is full of stories of last-minute speakers stealing the show. (The Watergate era alone provided numerous anecdotes of fund-raising events that had to be canceled or changed at the last minute due to certain actions taken against scheduled guest speakers.) If you are open about your problems, you can create press and interest. It won't work forever, but once or twice you can get away with attracting attention by making guests and press wonder just what exactly it is they will see or hear. Ways to acknowledge the problem while stirring up excitement in the press include announcements such as these:

- "Senator indicted but show will go on."
- "Accident causes change in schedule."
- "Hot Line Committee promises surprises at their fund-raising event."

Natural Calamities

Natural calamities, such as fires or snowstorms, are perfect excuses to get that special press release out about your event and increase interest in it. An important psychological trigger for charitable giving is based on the sense that someone is in need. Fire, flood, snowstorm, or some other kind of outside disaster can be used as a strong pull as people empathize with your plight and respond to your need. Develop this positive attitude in your press:

- "Neither snowstorm nor snowstorm will stop this event."
- "Ice Skating Rink Project able to obtain immortal classic *Gone With the Wind* screening to be highlight of benefit." (If your outside party is forced to move indoors.)
- "Mayor to read special telegrams by celebrity guests." (If your celebrity guest speakers can't get in.)

If All Else Fails . . .

The last resort is always there: You can abandon the project. If your special event just will not sell, if you can't get the program together you promised people, if your expenses have run out of control, if all your efforts to redeem the situation fail, it may be necessary to call it quits.

If you come to this painful decision, don't shrink away in embarrassment. Instead, be straightforward and open about what has happened and why you feel this is now the best course to take. Explain that not enough tickets were sold, and the primary purpose of the event, after all, is not to have a party but to get a twenty-four-hour hot line started. Many people will be sympathetic and let you keep the money. (Remember, it is a 100 percent deductible contribution, whether or not there is an event attached to it.) Let this problem prove that if nothing else your organization is fiscally responsible, and best yet, let the world at large and your supporters see that you are ready to learn from this last-ditch plan to abandon the event. It is not the end of the world but just an unfortunate detour that will lead to a new informed beginning.

* * *

Of all fund-raising methods, special events are the most obvious (because of their public nature) places where troubleshooting is needed. When you stub your toe with a special event, it is usually in front of a great number of your friends or people who will soon be former friends. It is only one area among many within the fund-raising arena in which troubleshooting is vital. A more insidious, subtle area in which to troubleshoot is within your organization itself.

Organizations

I realize that many of you may not have an organization yet. You may be one person with only an idea at this moment and having a staff and a formalized structure may seem an impossible dream. First of all, realize that having a staff does not by itself make things easier and can even complicate matters in certain ways.

A large part of the work for Minnesota Science Museum of St. Paul director Jim Peterson is to filter through and organize staff ideas before actually being able to fund raise. As he described it in the April 1986 issue of *Twin Cities* magazine:

> We have many creative people with loads of bright ideas. My job is to organize those ideas, put them into a museum context, then put together the resources needed to see them through.

Although this discussion may not pertain to your present situation, I suggest you remember it because someday you may very well become formally organized, and the roots of most funding problems can be found within the organizational structure itself. Almost all of the problems that require special event troubleshooting could have been avoided if organizational problems had been uncovered and resolved first. Most of the problems that will be discussed later in the chapter concerning direct mail, corporate, and foundation fund-raising are outgrowths of basic, fundamental organizational problems.

What are some of these problems?

Confusion Over Goals

What they are and what they should be. Confusion arises when project goals overshadow the larger goals that the project was set up for. Rushing to conclusions without first thoroughly analyzing the problem at hand may lead to an inappropriate or inadequate solution. Take the project goals we've been using as models: to build an ice skating rink, to start a twenty-four-hour hot line, to fund a trip to Washington, D.C., for seniors. Out of context like this, it is impossible to make any kind of definitive judgments of these project goals, but these are the kind of questions and the sort of thinking process that should have gone on before we settled on these goals:

OUR GOAL: To do something about the unstructured leisure time of our youth. (Remember, our goal is not to build an ice skating rink. That's our project goal.)

QUESTION: Is it an ice skating rink that needs to be built or would the youth of our community be better served by constructing a crafts center on the site that could be used in the summertime when they are really at loose ends?

OUR GOAL: To curb the growing rate of suicide among teenagers.

QUESTION: Are we starting the hot line just to be able to say we are doing something, or does a much larger effort need to take place to eradicate the problem?

OUR GOAL: To make living conditions better for seniors.

QUESTION: Is sending a group of seniors to lobby for their rights in Congress the best course of action, or would it be more beneficial to do something ourselves about their living conditions in our community?

It doesn't hurt to examine and reinforce your goal, not only for your volunteers and supporters but also for your public. Often, you can get so caught up in the fund-raising that you lose sight of what the fund-raising is for.

Leadership

Who is running this organization or this project fund drive? What is the chain of authority and responsibility? It is helpful to draw up a simple organizational chart that can be given to new members of your board or volunteer group. Occasionally, corporate and foundation sources might want to see such a chart also. The organizational chart for a new project fund drive might be as simple as this:

Project Responsibilities Chart
Senior Trip Project

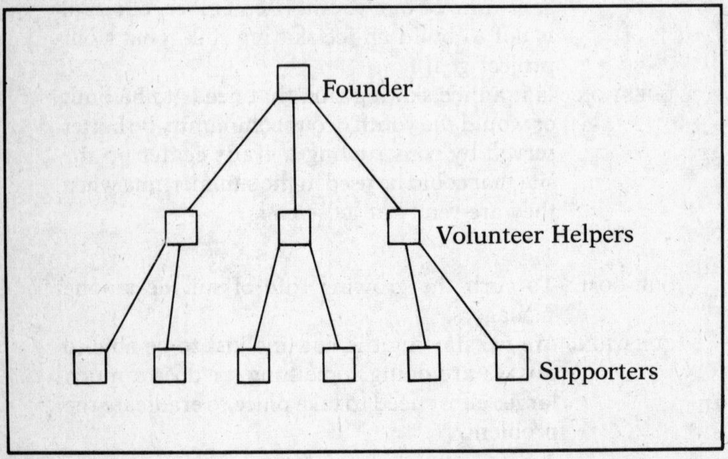

This is not to say that this hierarchy is the standard. Many of the best nonprofit ideas see the original organizer stepping aside or becoming a member of the volunteer group as the idea starts to form itself into an organization:

Organizational Responsibilities Chart
Senior Supports, Inc.

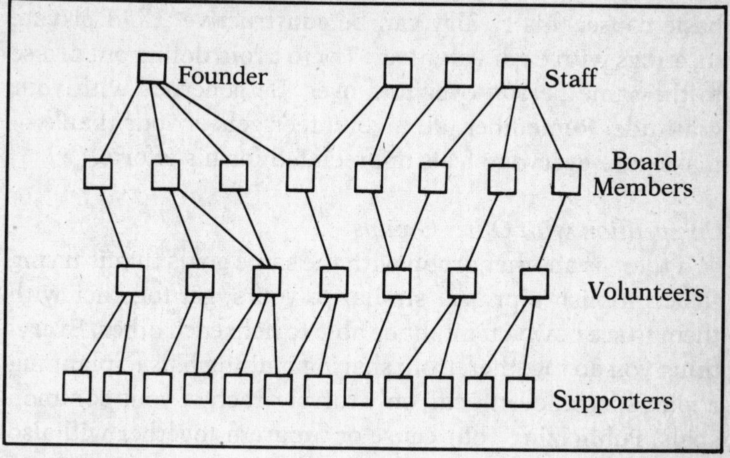

Work Load

One of the most common organizational problems is the mismanagement of people power. Your staff and volunteers are your most valuable resources in any fund-raising campaign. Get to know them and understand what they can and cannot do. At that first organizational meeting, find out what each volunteer's schedule is like. How much time can they afford to give you? Take all this information into serious consideration as you plan your strategy. Don't plan an extensive door-to-door campaign if all your volunteers work forty to sixty hours a week. Be flexible. Don't get stuck on an idea that may prove unworkable because of an unrealistic distribution of duties.

Rivalries Within the Group

If you have ten people helping you raise money, some of them will be more successful than the others. The rivalry that can develop can be destructive if it leads to a defeatist attitude or hostility within the group. If it is viewed as healthy competition with everyone pulling together for the same basic cause, this rivalry can be constructive. Hold private meetings with each volunteer. Try to avoid doling out praise to the same person over and over. Be generous with your gratitude. Remember, all a volunteer gets is your thanks—make sure everyone feels appreciated for his efforts.

Competition with Other Groups

If there is another group with the same goals that is trying to accomplish a project similar to yours, get together with them to see how you might be able to help each other. Everything you do together, from sharing mailing lists to planning a joint special event, can only further each of your common goals. Publicizing your cause or program together will also emphasize to the general public the urgency and scope of this common concern. Above all, don't knock the competition—you may have much to gain from it.

Burnout

A term born in the seventies that has even more application in the materialistic eighties, "burnout" can cause real damage to your fund-raising efforts. Volunteers have different energy levels, and some may succumb to burnout before your drive is completed. It is a good idea to keep the door open at all times to new volunteers, fresh troops that can relieve your helpers. Be on guard against burnout in yourself as well. No matter how important the cause, no matter how urgent the need for which you're fund-raising, don't overlook your own needs. Working ninety hours a week will do no one any good if you are not able to follow your project through to the end.

Direct Mail

Direct-mail campaigns have become as much a part of all our lives as newspaper ads and TV and radio commercials. As consumers, some of us respond better than others to this form of advertising, due to a variety of personality characteristics. (For instance, some beer drinkers like ex-jocks telling them it "tastes great"; others don't. That's advertising psychology, folks.) As fund-raisers conducting a direct-mail campaign, we want to increase this level of response.

We'll never get a 100 percent positive response to a direct-mail campaign, but we should at the very least get 2 percent, and with a personalized list (as described in Chapter 4), this percentage should rise close to 20 percent. If this isn't happening, your return percentage is lower than it should be. Take a look at some factors that might be behind this low rate of response:

The Letter Itself

The Fund-Raising Institute conducts a "Letter Clinic" to teach students to analyze direct-mail letters in terms of their potential success rate. FRI's president William Bathaser gave these fund-raising tips in a February 1986 article on direct-mail campaigning:

• Is your need clear? Does the reader have to get through more than one paragraph before knowing why the letter is being written?

• Have you put your emphasis in such a way (using underlining, heavier graphics, italics, capital letters, and so on) that the reader gets a sense of the letter even by skimming? (Sadly, that's what most of us do when we get direct mail.)

• Have you asked the reader questions that will keep his or her interest? Do you follow the story of the letter along or does the letter start and stop?

• Is your summary also clear? Does the person getting the

letter know what to do to help? (Use enclosed envelope, send check to, call this number immediately, and so on.)

Review the seven key elements of a successful fund-raising letter that we discussed earlier. To reiterate:

Key Elements of a Successful Fund-raising Letter

- Describe the sender.
- Describe the reader.
- Establish the need for help.
- Pinpoint that need (your goal).
- State the project budget.
- Lay out the timeline for the drive.
- Describe how effectiveness of the drive will be measured.

If your letter is missing any of these parts, take another look to see how you can work in that missing information.

It is not unheard of to do a follow-up letter, in fact, direct-mail follow-up is part of the traditional approach to fund-raising. To reinforce the "Show Me" motivation if your drive is not doing well, you might add something new to what you are already offering your potential givers. The follow-up letter should be different from your first letter but related enough to be clearly seen as a follow-up to the same appeal. The follow-up letter could be basically a reworking of the original letter with an opening paragraph similar to the following:

> Dear ____________:
>
> A month ago we sent you and 199 other individuals a letter describing why we need a twenty-four-hour suicide hot line in Centerville. Eleven individuals have responded so far and have been invited to a very special evening with State Senator ____________ and Mayor ____________ to discuss what we can do as individuals to curb the growing problem of teenage suicide. We have not yet heard

> from you. If you were planning on responding but haven't yet, would you consider giving now? We'd like to have you join us for this important panel, and when you use the enclosed SASE, we'll send you your invitation to join Mayor __________ and State Senator __________.
>
> (If you've misplaced our original letter, here is what we are all about. . . .

The rest of the letter would then cover the same seven points outlined in the original letter but using different wording.

The follow-up letter does not have to be restricted to a reworking of your original letter. Alternative methods of follow-ups to boost a sagging campaign or increase the response even further on a booming one include:

- A letter from a supporter.

"Dear Friend, I wanted to take this opportunity to tell you why I sent $25 to support the seniors' trip from our community to Washington, D.C. . . ."

- Testimonial from well-known people in support of your idea. (Or even not so well known. If they are not recognizable names, identify them by profession, i.e., teacher, homemaker, writer, policeman, and so on.)
- Clippings from the press stressing the urgency of support for your idea (or a similar one), reporting another community's success with a like project.
- Photos that bring to life the urgency of meeting the need you're raising funds for (i.e., children skating on a pond next to a sign reading DANGER: THIN ICE illustrates the need for an ice skating rink very clearly.)
- Personalized notes from you or members of your committee written across the edge of a copy of the original letter, i.e., "I'm not sure if you saw this the first time we sent it" or "Thanks for taking the time to look at this letter again."

Combining direct mail with telephoning is a clear-cut and fairly easy way to troubleshoot. Within two to three weeks after the letters go out, get on the phone to at least part of the mailing list and ask questions. Are they not giving because they forgot about the letter? Are they saying they have no money? Are they confused? Keep track of their responses. Before abandoning direct mail, try to get a sense of why it is not working as well as you had planned. You may find a way to remedy the situation in your follow-up.

If follow-ups aren't working and if phoning people directly isn't giving you a clear idea of what the problem is, then look at your mailing list. A friend mailed 20,000 letters last year for a children's science museum project only to discover a month after the mailing went out that her word processor had inserted the number nine wherever the number two was supposed to be on all the mailing labels. Do you have correct up-to-date addresses? Test mail first-class letters (which will be returned if addresses are incorrect) to a few people you haven't heard from to find out if the list is reliable.

A nice thing about conducting a direct-mail campaign is that you should be able to count on a certain percentage of response. If you've written a good letter and have a good mailing list, you will get something. Make sure your goals are set ahead of time and be ready to go back to work if those goals are not being met.

If you've done all your double checking and revising and adding on, and you still aren't coming up with a 20 percent response, it's time to broaden your horizons. Pull out your second shopping list (the one with names of people with whom you have no direct contact but who seem—i.e., due to location, profession, age—likely prospects) to support your project and send out a mailing to them.

If you have the happily unsettling situation of having your goals met faster than you anticipated, congratulations—you have a good combination of the right letter and a great mailing list. However, still consider doing follow-up and other troubleshooting. Why not see if you can be the one to hit that mythical fund-raiser's dream of the 100 percent response?

Corporations and Foundations

You've mailed off the proposal. The fate of your project lies in the hands of the corporate or foundation decision-makers. Now, all you can do is hope for the best and wait until you hear from them. Sounds pretty clear-cut, but you can take action to alleviate anxiety and strengthen your case further during this "wait and hear" period that will improve your situation whatever the outcome.

First of all, it is helpful to understand the way in which corporations and foundations make their funding decisions. Most have a committee of anywhere from three to thirty people who review proposals. Usually, these groups (especially the larger committees) depend upon staff recommendations to help them make these decisions. These committees do not meet weekly. Once you have had your meeting and/or submitted your proposal, it can take anywhere from three weeks to a year to get a response. Try to find out in your research or at your meeting how long this wait should be. Be patient and don't expect a decision faster than what is given as the minimum period of response. If the funding source takes six to eight weeks to review a proposal, wait, say, ten weeks before calling to make inquiries.

You don't have to remain totally in the dark until you get the final word, however. Careful research of the corporation's funding policies and procedures, along with asking them point-blank about your chances at the initial and any subsequent meetings, should give you a fair idea of what to expect.

When you do call, be polite. Don't force the issue. If it appears that your proposal has been lost, then hand deliver (if possible) another one immediately. Don't blame anyone for the loss; just get another proposal to them while they are feeling slightly guilty.

If you phone and still are confused about when your proposal will be reviewed and when you can reasonably expect an answer, then write a note asking for an update on your proposal. Occasionally, the note will lead the funding source to discover that your proposal has been misplaced or forgotten, and such a note will get you back toward the top of the pile.

During the waiting period, you might get a call asking questions about your proposal (especially if you didn't get a chance to meet with a staff member). If the call comes, suggest scheduling a meeting to discuss the questions. If that is not possible, then suggest you send in the answers in written form, which allows a bit more time to think through your response and compose your thoughts succinctly. If, however, you are finally requested to respond over the phone, do so. Remember, the staff person is trying his or her best to represent your proposal well, so help by being as clear and concise as possible.

When you do get the response to your proposal and find it's a negative one, is there anything you can do? One appropriate action you can—and should—take is to try to find out *why* your request for funding was turned down. If your meeting or subsequent conversations with the staff of the foundation or corporation had led you to believe you would get some support, feel free to call and ask what happened.

Again, don't be pushy. If the staff person can't give you reasons over the phone, ask if he or she might want to reply in writing at his or her convenience. Study their reasons for the rejection of your proposal and use them to write another proposal. (Unless you are told directly not to bother to reapply—and this does happen.) Remember that private foundations and corporations are just that—private. They don't owe you anything. It is your job—not theirs—to prove a need and gain support for that need.

Another thing. No matter what your private feelings toward a funding source, don't be public about them. An organization or an individual with a reputation for bad-mouthing a donor that turned them down is avoided like the plague by other potential donors. Corporations give money to help enhance their standing and image in the community and will stay away from groups that might try to damage that image in any way.

In any case, don't let a rejection throw you. Don't get paralyzed by it. You can often turn a bad situation into a good one by using it—whatever it may be—to your advantage. As always, be sure you have backup plans ready. If your proposal is turned down by one corporation, move on to the next name on your shopping list and submit to them. To speed things up and to dramatize your position as well, you can use the first rejection as bait: i.e., "We were expecting to get $______ from XYZ Corp., but it didn't work out. Can we meet quickly with you to see if ABC Corp. might be interested in our project?"

If you can't seem to get grant support for your project this time around, try to increase the take from the other parts of your funding scheme to make up the gap. Again, instead of hiding the fact that your proposal was unsuccessful, use this to your advantage. For example: You can raise ticket prices to your special event, saying publicly that it is because you did not get an expected grant. Likewise, this rationale can be the basis for the kickoff to a special "Fill the Gap" drive.

* * *

Whatever problems you may encounter in your quest to raise funds, try to keep a positive attitude. If your efforts to get things back on an even keel backfire and you have a disaster on your hands, deal with it as best you can. Don't leave town without a forwarding address. Be honest and open about your problems. Seek out the press and your supporters before they begin looking for you. Have your records in order and be ready to open your books to public scrutiny if your fund-raising has not met its goals and there is a question about whether your project will be able to go forward.

Remember, there is always a next time. By adopting a straightforward approach, you'll have a much better chance of getting the backing from your supporters and the media on your next venture because they'll know that you can be trusted. Whatever you can learn from mistakes made now will be invaluable to your troubleshooting and ultimate success in the future.

Resource List: Chapter 6

The numbers of publications dealing with corporate and foundation appeals and troubleshooting are almost limitless. Here are some that I find most useful:

How to Write Successful Corporate Appeals, With Full Examples
by James P. Sinclair
Public Service Materials Center
5130 MacArthur Boulevard, N.W.
Washington, D.C. 20016

The Experience of Smaller Nonprofits: Raising Money from Minnesota's Largest Foundations
by Frederick W. Smith and Rosangelica Aburto
The Center for Urban and Regional Affairs
330 Humphrey Center
301 Nineteenth Avenue South
Minneapolis, Minnesota 55455

Foundation News
published by
The Council on Foundations
1828 L Street, N.W.
Washington, D.C. 20036

Foundation Grants Index Bimonthly
published by
The Foundation Center
79 Fifth Avenue, Box CE
New York, New York 10003

chapter 7

FOLLOW-UP

"Charity," Mr. Hilton told his foundation board in his will, "is a supreme virtue, and the great channel through which the mercy of God is passed onto mankind."

—*The New York Times,* June 18, 1986

This directive may have helped save the day for 169 charities that were earmarked to receive the bulk of Conrad Hilton's multimillion-dollar estate but were faced with fervent opposition by the hotel magnate's children. In what could be called "follow-up from the grave," Mr. Hilton made it very clear how his philanthropic philosophy was to be carried out after his death. Without this clear stipulation in his will, those 169 charities may have ended up out in the cold.

The same sort of diligence about follow-up is essential at every step of the fund-raising process. Follow-up can be the most creative part of fund-raising because if done correctly, it leads to ongoing support and a very high level of goodwill. Your givers can become your spokespersons if they are handled right. On the other hand, lack of follow-up or inappropriate follow-up can be disastrous, no matter how successful a project is initially.

Fourteen "Do's and Don'ts"

Following is a list of "do's and don'ts" to ensure that your follow-up is both adequate and appropriate:

1. Do remember to thank people. It may seem obvious, but one of the biggest blunders fund-raisers make is not taking the time to thank people. And by "people," we don't just mean individual volunteers or contributors. Whether it is a corporation or foundation or a city or county agency, there are people within these institutions who helped your drive—find out who they are and let them know of your appreciation.

And do thank more than the person who actually gave you the grant. Especially with corporations and foundations, even if you never met the president or chairman of the board, still send them a thank-you. Include in these thank-yous some sort of tangible evidence of their gift—a magazine article or program that mentions the company name, a special letter of thanks that acknowledges their support. Send a formal thank-you to the president or chairman of the corporation and a less-formal note of appreciation can go to the individual who actually made the donation possible.

If you thank people verbally for donations received during a special event or a door-to-door campaign, be sure to follow up with a written thank-you. Whether or not you have thanked people in person, always take the time to send a thank-you letter. (It does not have to be an individualized letter for each person—by inserting the recipient's name and address, you can personalize thank-you letters in a minimum amount of time.)

Here is a copy of a thank-you letter that does a great job of follow-up that should ensure a sold-out event the next time around.

June 11, 1986

B.D. Carson
841 N. Stone St.
Culver City, CA

Dear Mr. Carson:

I wish to personally thank you for your presence at the Philippines event on May 7.

> Oxfam America raised nearly $2,000 dollars from donations during the evening and also received a check for $50,000 from a private foundation. We are really encouraged by this response.
>
> As of June 9, Oxfam America has approved $305,000 for emergency feeding on the island of Negros. Our hope is to raise one million dollars to fund long-term develop-ment projects in rural Philippines by the end of the year. My sincere gratitude for your support.
>
> Warm regards,
>
> Graciela Italiano
> New York Associate

2. Do be sure to send a receipt. No matter how bleak the government support of nonprofits becomes, people (and companies) will always be able to write off at least a part of their nonprofit gifts. Help them out. Make up a simple receipt and mail it out with your thank-you notes. (If you use a double-entry bookkeeping system—i.e., a carbon—you can also use your receipts as a simple record book for contributions.)

Here is an example of a receipt that any office supply or five-and-dime store supplies:

Sample Receipt

Received from: ______________________________ the sum of: $__________ for: contribution to the ______ ______________________________ (Tax deductible to full extent provided by law.)

3. Do send along gifts. Say that your drive is completed and your goal was met—the seniors' group is in Washington,

D.C., and plans are under way to create an ongoing senior support group in your community. How about sending a souvenir from Washington to everyone who helped make the trip possible? All congresspeople have pens or photos or some sort of giveaway that they'd be happy to donate to your cause. An unexpected gift can go a long way in increasing goodwill toward your current and future efforts.

4. Do be gracious, even if you don't make your goal. One of the most destructive pieces of P.R. that I have ever seen about the nonprofit world came out in all the major New York papers a few years ago. It concerned a theater company that had gotten less than expected from five corporations and thus was in danger of canceling an annual festival of new plays. The company called a reporter who wrote an article "damning" the funding community, which caused a lot of bad blood for all of us. The press was harmful enough to the theater involved, but it was disastrous for all of us working in the nonprofit field, as it gave the very strong impression that the corporations in question had reneged on their responsibility (and this at a time of severe crunches in a variety of corporate fields).

By my way of thinking, just about anyone is a potential future supporter. No matter how disappointed you may feel, don't offend those who did support you or who might well support you in the future.

5. Do remember to list your contributors in programs, annual reports, press releases, and so on. The gratification of seeing one's name appear among a list of supporters is one of the first tenets of a "Show Me" approach to fund-raising. So often, once the drive is over and the goal is met, we tend to lose sight of how important this follow-up to our efforts really is. A general rule of thumb is to keep on listing your contributors for at least twelve months after the gift is actually given. The unlisted contributor is a serious oversight—he or she just may be sure to overlook you next year in return.

Here's an example of a nonprofit group that does monthly updates in their journal:

DONATIONS

CASH ($25.00 to $49.99)
Alex J. Barna, Media, PA
Donald L. Carmody, Huntington Beach, CA
Golden Eagle Coin Exchange, Adelphi, MD

CASH ($50.00 to $99.99)
Albuquerque World Coin, Albuquerque, NM

CASH ($100.00 to $299.99)
Al Adams Rare Coins, Atlanta, GA
American Coin Company, Studio City, CA
Garden State Numismatic Association, Toms River, NJ
Alan Kreuzer, Arcadia, CA
Utah Numismatic Society, Salt Lake City, UT

CASH ($300.00 to $499.99)
Little & Associates, Atlanta, GA

CASH ($500.00 to $999.99)
Oakland Coin Exchange, Inc., Oakland, CA
S.G. Rare Coins, Union, NJ

MATERIAL ($25.00 to $49.99)
Liberty Mint, Provo, UT

MATERIAL ($50.00 to $99.99)
William J. Bauer, Blue Island, IL

MATERIAL ($100.00 to $299.99)
Johnny H. Heleva, Citrus Heights, CA
Robert Lloyd, Florence, CO
Thomas P. McKenna, Ft. Collins, CO
Charles K. Mervine, Norristown, PA

MATERIAL ($300.00 to $499.99)
Frank S. Robinson, Albany, NY

MATERIAL (no stated value)
Carnegie Coin Club, Hatfield, MA
Francis Contino, Philadelphia, PA
The Franklin Mint, Franklin Center, PA
James B. Grotberg, Chicago, IL
Jerome H. Remick, Ste.-Foy, Quebec, Canada
John Paul Sarosi, Johnstown, PA
Arthur P. Tuberman, Lake Havasu City, AZ
Washington-Montgomery-Prince Georges Tri-Club, Tuscarora, MD
M.E. Zubatkin, Clifton, NJ

Total Cash
$25 or more $2,300.00
Less than $25 ....93.95
Total Material 1,333.75
Total Donations (6-30-86) $3,727.70

1858 THE NUMISMATIST

On the other hand, there are some people (and some corporations and foundations) who don't want their name to be used or even listed. You should always obtain permission first from people or companies before using their names. If nothing else, a postscript on your formal thank-you notes can accomplish the job.

For example:

> P.S. We would like to include your name on our list of "Angels." Please let us know if you have any objection.

Also be sure to inquire how the contributor would like to be listed. An addition to the above postscript can provide this information:

> Is the way your name is printed on this letter how you would like to be listed in our annual report?

6. Do put out a press release listing the names of major (or if the drive is small enough, all) donors who do not wish to remain anonymous. Many smaller newspapers will let you write your own article—if you are given this opportunity, seize it. Use any chance you can to thank supporters in print for their gifts.

7. Don't misuse your contributors' gifts. If you say you will use contributions to pay for the lumber for the ice skating rink, make sure that is what you use the funds for. One of the most common problems in nonprofit fund-raising is not being able to carry through with your announced intentions.

What happens if you don't raise enough funds to build that ice skating rink? Be honest with your supporters. Write or phone them and explain the situation. Ask them if you can keep their gift until the drive is completed or if they will allow you to use their contribution for another purpose. Just be sure you communicate with your supporters before they read about your failure to build the ice skating rink in the local newspaper—or, worse yet, hear it from other supporters.

8. Don't immediately ask for money again after you've gotten your first gift. Unless there is a pressing reason (i.e., your group has a chance to perform in East Germany; your

building does not pass fire inspection) and unless it has been made very clear that you'll be asking again soon, it is generally best to wait a year before approaching the same people for support monies again. Urgent appeals lose their sense of urgency if done too often. In the world of fund-raising, the too-oft-cried urgent appeal is akin to the boy shouting "Wolf" a few too many times.

9. Do keep in touch with your supporters. Just because you aren't asking for money for a year doesn't mean your contributors should not hear from you during this time. Your goal is to convert new friends into loyal supporters and to keep longtime supporters loyal. And follow-up is the key to making this goal.

Keep your current and past supporters updated on your activities. Send them the press release that announces the successful end of your drive. Send them newspaper clippings about your project. Send them copies of thank-you letters from people being served by your program. If nothing else, send them another thank-you. One of my favorite techniques is to do an end of the year wrap-up letter that updates givers on the progress of our program (i.e., their money). These letters invariably bring in extra unsolicited contributions just because of the gratitude people feel toward this special consideration. They also can be used to help update would-be donors who are still "on the fence."

10. Don't be pushy. When the time comes to solicit past contributors a second time and no gift is forthcoming, don't push too hard to get a second gift. I personally despise the letters that start off pleading, "We haven't heard from you yet this year. What happened?" Even worse are the letters with the belligerent tone: "Last year you gave. Why not this year?" Remember, many individuals (and all corporations and foundations) are on a budget that only allows them to give a certain amount to nonprofit organizations each year. For whatever reason they may only give once to your cause,

don't push them for more. Using the soft-soap approach we discussed earlier, in which you keep updating them on your progress and so on, is not offensive to anyone and will be far more effective in promoting your cause.

Don't forget that your contributors—past or present—are your friends. They believe in what you are doing. Don't turn them off. Even if they don't give again, keep them feeling good about what you are doing. Word of mouth is the best friend any nonprofit idea can have. Bad word of mouth is very difficult to overcome and can severely damage your entire operation.

11. Don't get overconfident. The most disappointing direct-mail campaign I ran started off way ahead of every past drive. At the end of our first month, we had almost doubled the take from the same point the previous year. We started to become complacent and backed off on our follow-up work. Ultimately, the drive never reached its goal.

12. Share your lists in moderation. Some fund-raisers believe you should never reveal your sources of contributions for fear other groups will spirit them away from you. I'm a great believer in developing the best possible shopping list of potential contributors, and I think one of the best techniques to accomplish this is to trade mailing lists with other organizations with goals similar to yours. Just keep this trading reasonable. No one wants to give money to your group, only to be flooded by appeals from dozens of other groups.

13. Do utilize the resources of your supporters. In addition to financial contributions to your organization, your supporters may be happy to work with you in other ways. Remember them when adding to your volunteer list, your board of directors, special committees, and so on. Very often new supporters are eager to get involved with the nonprofit organization they have chosen to support. Without being pushy, give them a chance to increase their commitment.

14. Do use the supporters of your current drive to help in the planning of your next drive, whether or not the first drive has been successful. A simple questionnaire conducted by mail, over the phone, or door-to-door can tell you more about your givers than any number of books or studies or outside consultant's reports. Some of the questions that you should be asking your supporters include:

Were you happy to give to this drive?
How do you like to be asked for money?
How much do you give in any one year?
Up to $100 __________
Up to $500 __________
Up to $1,000 __________
Over $1,000 __________
What suggestions do you have for us?
Would you like to help in other ways?

If I seem to be giving the impression that contributors are rare and delicate creatures who must be treated with sensitivity, I am. It is much easier to keep a contributor happy, involved, and giving than to find a replacement for that person. As a rule of thumb, you should expect to lose between 8 and 12 percent of your givers each year for a variety of reasons (economic problems, relocation, varying choices of recipients, and so on). If the percentage of loss rises any higher, I suggest you review the "do's and don'ts" list with care.

Just as you are analyzing your contributors' responses to your funding techniques, get the reactions of other members of the organization. It is much easier to analyze a drive as soon as it ends—when you have time to breathe—than to wait until the start of the next one—when you won't have this luxury of time to conduct analysis. Get your group together for a question-and-answer period and record the responses either on paper in report form or on tape. Examples of the type of questions to be asking include:

- Where did we have troubles with our drive?
- What felt good about what we did?
- What didn't feel so good?
- What suggestions did people make as we were actually conducting the drive?
- What suggestions can we make looking back on it all?
- Was the shopping list a good one?
- Were the goals attainable?
- Were the goals too low? (A more common problem than you might think.)
- Do we have the committee's respect and interest and will we be ready for our next drive?
- What questions should we have asked before that we are asking now?

Make sure that you deal with all aspects of your fund-raising efforts—not just the financial ones but the promotional and personal aspects as well. Nothing is sadder than a new nonprofit idea bursting onto the scene that no one hears about or that burns out all the volunteers before things really get into gear.

In addition to the questionnaires, nothing is more helpful in planning future fund-raising projects than the information gleaned from past project analyses. Make up a concise final report form to aid your analysis. This form can also be used to report back to your volunteer committee or board of directors and/or to a corporation or foundation that gave you a challenge grant or is interested in seeing the results of your drive. Below is a sample final report form that can be altered to fit most circumstances and, most importantly, can be easily used as a springboard for your next year's projected fund drive budget. There is no better way to develop your next budget than by seeing what the exact costs were the year before.

Sample Final Report

INCOME	
Tickets sold	$25,440.00 (424 @ $60 each)
Contributions	9,120.00
Pledges	1,275.00
Journal ads	7,000.00
TOTAL INCOME:	$42,835.00
EXPENSES	
Dinners served	$ 8,748.00 (486 @ $18 each)
Bottles of wine served (corkage)	2,640.00 (264 @ $10 each)
Gratuities	2,085.60 (17% + beverage)
Checkroom	345.70
Soda	99.10
Amplification	75.00
Postage	500.00
Invitation (layout, printing, cards, envelopes)	579.63
Clerical help	218.75
Stationery Supplies	12.00
Printing (table lists)	65.50
Messenger service	50.00
Publicist	125.00
Miscellaneous (cabs, car rental, parking tips, press sandwiches)	310.54
TOTAL EXPENSES	$15,854.82
NET PROFIT:	$27,945.18

The assumption throughout this book has been that most new ideas will either be absorbed by an existing nonprofit agency or institution or they will create a new nonprofit entity to be formed around them. If an idea is a viable one that the community will support during a fund drive to get the project going, there needs to be a structure set up to ensure the ongoing operations of that project—i.e., the maintenance of the ice skating rink, the manning of the hot line, the self-help group for seniors. The key to forming such a nonprofit group is the board of directors. These are the people who agree to make a longer term commitment to your project than just the one fund drive. If you have worn out these volunteer board members during this initial drive and you have to seek new people all over again to join your cause, the first few years of your program will be rocky indeed. Be sure to treat your people well. They are your most valuable assets.

Some very good books have been written about developing nonprofit institutions, boards of directors, and so on. At the end of each chapter, a few of these books have been listed. If your idea has grown to the point that you want to consider permanence in the form of a nonprofit institution, I strongly recommend reading one or more of these books.

A Last Word

Before we part company and you go off to tackle your own specific fund-raising challenges, I feel obligated to insert a note of caution in the form of a *New York Times* editorial from August 6, 1986, when Congress was working hard on coming up with tax revisions to cut down on the ability of individuals to deduct nonprofit donations from their taxes.

Hard Times for Charity

By Brian O'Connell

Triple whammy for nonprofits

WASHINGTON — For six years President Reagan and Congress have called on nonprofit organizations to expand their services to replace Government programs, while at the same time reducing Government support for these charitable groups. Now they are getting ready to strike another serious blow against nonprofit organizations by altering the tax provisions that encourage citizens to contribute their money and property.

Analysts estimate that the new tax bill would automatically reduce charitable giving by about $6 billion a year, or about 8 percent, because lower tax rates would make charitable deductions less attractive. What's worse, though, unless the House and Senate tax committee conferees restore certain provisions, another $7 billion could be lost, because under the Senate version of the bill taxpayers who do not itemize their returns would no longer be allowed to deduct charitable contributions, and because under the House version deductions of gifts of appreciated property would be less valuable.

If all of this were to occur, we would have a situation where Government says to the voluntary agencies, in effect: "We are looking to you to make up for our cutbacks and the increased service needs they cause, but we are cutting back on our share of the partnership and, by the way, we are undermining your contributed support in the range of 15 to 20 percent."

The $6 billion loss from lower rates is something we are going to have to accept as part of the price of tax reform. The other $7 billion loss is something we in the nonprofit sector cannot live with.

People donate money to help other people, causes and communities, but the size of charitable gifts is influenced by the ability to deduct them. According to Treasury Department findings, when the top tax rate dropped in 1981 from 70 percent to 50 percent, charitable giving declined among people with incomes above $50,000. For those who earn incomes of $100,000 to $200,000, it dropped during the

Brian O'Connell is president of Independent Sector, an organization that encourages support for nonprofit institutions.

next two years by 17 percent, and for those in the $200,000-to-$500,000 range, it dropped 35 percent.

Fortunately, that large loss was overcome by more giving from people with incomes below $30,000 whose charitable support was stimulated by the approval, also in 1981, of deductions for those who do not itemize.

In 1986 we are faced with an equally large rate reduction, repeal of the deduction clause for those who do not itemize and continued expectations for expanded service. That's a devastating triple whammy. Charitable giving is expanding, but it is not keeping pace with the decline in the Government's share of the cost of providing services.

The Urban Institute recently published a report including a five-year analysis of the impact on nonprofit organizations of Federal budget cuts and projections for the next three years. The report says: "The reductions in Federal spending recently proposed by the Reagan Administration in its budget for fiscal years 1987-89 would place serious strains on the thousands of health clinics, day care centers, employment and training programs, social service providers, colleges, research institutes, neighborhood groups and other organizations that comprise the nation's private, nonprofit sector. . . . These proposed cuts come on top of prior reductions in Federal spending in fields where nonprofits are active."

The report concludes: "Far from being able to expand their services to meet the increased demand left by Government cutbacks, many nonprofit organizations consequently found it difficult to maintain even their prior level of services."

It is a matter of fairness and common sense for the Senate conferees to accept the House tax provision that allows the continuation of charitable deductions for non-itemizers. That would restore $6 billion of annual contributions. Also, the House conferees should accept the Senate's version allowing continued deduction of gifts of appreciated property. That would restore another $1 billion.

With luck, in a couple of years we can make up the inevitable loss of $6 billion that we must endure. Any larger loss, however, would be cruel treatment for anyone who relies on voluntary agencies for assistance. □

Before this book went to press, the apprehensions expressed by Mr. O'Connell unfortunately turned into realities. With the passage of the Tax Reform Act of 1986, charitable giving by individuals and corporations has been severely affected in three major ways:

1. Tax rates have been lowered, thus reducing the value of charitable deductions.
2. Deductions for charitable contributions have been eliminated for taxpayers who do not itemize. (In 1985 non-itemizers accounted for 64.4 percent of U.S. taxpayers, according to *The New York Times*.)
3. Donors of securities, artwork, real estate, and other assets that grow in value from their acquisition date will be required to add the amount their gift grew in value back into their income and may then be subject to the alternative minimum tax.

* * *

Again, according to *The New York Times*, Independent Sector estimates an annual loss of $11 billion in contributions to nonprofits from the first two features of the act and some tax analysts estimate another $1 billion loss from the third feature. And lawyers specializing in tax laws and charitable giving say we are only seeing the tip of the iceberg now.

"It's a monstrous law in terms of the negative impact it will have on fund-raising programs of charities," said Stanley S. Weithorn, a New York lawyer, talking before the National Health Council.

Before you succumb to doom and gloom, however, remember all you've just read. In spite of the fact that the big picture is, indeed, depressing, there is much—using the "Show Me" techniques—you can do to keep your organization alive and healthy.

The major criticism I've received in over fifteen years of professional fund-raising is that I'm too optimistic. Perhaps I seem that way at times, but I hope this book has convinced you that, using the "Show Me" approach to fund-raising, you too can be optimistic. There are new ways of asking for money that do not involve reliance on tax benefits.

The "Show Me" approach to fund-raising is not the panacea that will restore the billions that we have lost in the nonprofit sector due to government budget cuts and tax reform. The "Show Me" approach will, however, allow us to attract new dollars from new people. By giving something back to those who give to you, you develop a contributor who responds directly to you, not to forces which are out of your hands. As long as you can keep him motivated, as long as you can offer him a good reason to keep supporting your cause, you are in control of the situation. You are in control of your fund-raising.

If this book has made a believer out of you, if you are eager to get going on "Show Me" fund-raising—not just one time but again and again in the years to come—look through the references to other books, newsletters, services, magazines, and so on that will help you to learn more about this fascinating field of human endeavor.

Welcome to the world of fund-raising. It's not the easiest way to survive in this, the late eighties U.S.A., but if your idea is a good one, if—as the knights of old would say—your cause is just, then the new fund-raising is a challenging way to survive and to ultimately make our society a better place to live and work.

Resource List: Chapter 7

And the final list of further reading . . .

Evaluation Handbook
Public Management Institute
358 Brannan Street
San Francisco, California 84107

The Thirteen Most Common Fund-raising Mistakes and How to Avoid Them
by Paul H. Schneiter and Donald T. Nelson
Public Service Materials Center
5130 MacArthur Boulevard, N.W.
Washington, D.C. 20016

Planned Giving Idea Book
by Robert F. Sharpe
Thomas Nelson Publishers
Nashville, Tennessee 37202

APPENDIX A

Glossary

What Comes In and What Goes Out

Budget

A plan that details how you will bring in money (income) and how you will pay money out (expenses) over a specific period of time and/or for a specific project or program. No matter what type of fund-raising work you are engaging in, having both sides of the budget worked out so that they balance each other is essential.

Usually, the budget is created by studying past fund-raising performance, as well as conservative use of shopping lists.

Sample Project Budget

Income:	
Corporate	$2,500
Individual	2,000
Special Event	2,000
In-kind	500
TOTAL INCOME:	$7,000
Expenses:	
Project	$5,000
Fund-raising	1,000
Special Event	750
Miscellaneous	250
TOTAL EXPENSES:	$7,000

Sample Annual Budget for Organization

EXPENSES:

Personnel	
Staff Salaries	$133,817
Payroll Taxes	10,000
Employee Insurance	5,484
	149,301
Occupancy	
Mortgage	4,036
Insurance	4,912
Utilities	10,731
R&M and Supplies	5,515
	25,194

Program	
Workshop	13,904
Literary	18,522
Services	—
Executive Director	3,380
Playwrights' Travel	6,864
	42,670
Administrative and General	
Audit and Legal	2,691
Office Supplies	4,988
Printing and Duplicating	10,290
Postage	6,404
Telephone	10,159
Dues and Promotion	1,433
Special Promotion	—
Refreshments	3,468
Miscellaneous	5,498
	45,381
Fund-raising	
General	6,888
Industry Drive	2,686
Luncheon	22,904
	32,478
Total Operating:	$295,024
Capital Improvements:	$103,589
Endowment:	—
TOTAL EXPENSES:	$398,613

Income:

Contributions	
NEA/NYSCA Grants	$99,000
Foundations	80,500
Corporations	38,876
Industry Drive	36,381

Luncheon Proceeds	44,610
Luncheon Journal	
Capital Fund Drive	88,767
TOTAL CONTRIBUTIONS:	$388,134
Earned Income	
Rentals	2,524
Miscellaneous Classes	1,887
Scriptshare	5,700
TOTAL EARNED INCOME:	$10,111
TOTAL INCOME:	$398,245
Endowment	—
TOTAL REVENUES:	$398,245

What You Want

Money

There is no special mystery about money gotten through fund-raising. Money is money. It's what some individual or organization has that you need. Fund-raising is the craft of successfully getting the money.

Are there different kinds of money?

Yes. And this is where fund-raising starts to get interesting. Following are descriptions of the types of money most people fund-raise for:

GENERAL OPERATING SUPPORT

For many of you reading this book, this will be the kind of money you need to find. It is for the ongoing operations of your activity. Everything necessary for the maintenance of this activity—from money to help cover the costs of your monthly meetings to the printing of the newsletter announcing them—comes under this heading. You can get general operating support money through almost any means—

direct-mail campaigns, door-to-door drives, corporate grants, special events. It's what most people assume their dollars are going for when they give.

CAPITAL SUPPORT

These funds go towards acquiring, maintaining, and/or renovating tangibles, what foundations love to call "bricks and mortar" monies. If your meeting place needs a coat of paint, if your fieldhouse bathroom could use more modern plumbing, if you want to buy a decent typewriter for once and for all, you are looking for capital support.

Some foundations like to give capital support specifically. Individuals and corporations like to give to capital drives because the idea of helping to build something that is more or less permanent is very satisfying. If nothing else, as more than one reluctant donor has surely mumbled throughout history, "It's nice to see where the damn money is going." With capital monies you certainly can see what you paid for.

PROJECT MONIES

These are the most commonly asked for dollars from foundations and various government sources. You have an idea of how to solve a need? You want to try that idea once? There you have a special project.

It may be that you have a plan to transform a deserted lot full of garbage into a public sculpture garden or want to send the town's Girl Scout troop to Washington, D.C., to attend special congressional hearings on women's rights. Whatever the scope of your project, you need to find monies to cover the added costs to your budget of carrying out this project.

No matter how large or how small your organization is, you will soon discover that finding funds for these special projects is an ongoing need. Developing a donor pool or bank who will be responsive to new ideas as you come up with them is a real priority in your fund-raising plan. More about how to do that later. . . .

PROGRAM MONIES

These are more integral dollars as this type of support is for a project that is seen to be important enough to continue past the project stage. You may want to implement an "Adopt a Grandparent" program of weekly nursing home visitations by teenagers or incorporate a series of dance concerts for children in your company's annual schedule of performances. The programs are what make up the entire operation. You should be able to separate program budgets and needs from general operating.

It is a good idea to have a separate budget line for each program for two reasons: It is easier to raise money for an individual program when it is isolated from the on-going operations budget. Secondly, it is a sad fact of nonprofit life that when funds don't meet the budget's needs, sometimes programs have to be cut. Having a separate budget line for each program also makes it easier to accomplish this always painful task when necessary.

ENDOWMENT MONIES

Fund-raising for this type of support is an activity for the more sophisticated and established organization or idea. If you have supporters who are already convinced that what you are doing is important and should have a long life, then you are ready to start raising endowment monies, which go into a trust fund or secure bank account and operate essentially as an organization's insurance policy or savings account. Some of our most hallowed nonprofit institutions (colleges, museums, zoos) have endowments in the hundreds of millions of dollars. In times like this when the game of fund-raising is changing so quickly, an endowment is one of the few ways of ensuring an organization's stability.

How to Get What You Want

Proposal Writing

The most traditional method of fund-raising, in simplest terms, is the process of fund-raising done in written form. A proposal can be a 100-page document explaining what you need, why you need it, what you'll do with it once you get it, or it can be a 2-page letter that accomplishes the same thing.

In Chapter 3, we outlined what needs to go into an effective proposal. Again, the trepidation many people feel when faced with writing a proposal is really unwarranted. If you can write a friendly letter, you can write a proposal.

Drive

An organized attempt to raise monies for a specific need. Most of the descriptions of fund-raising efforts we have given in this book will fit into the category of a drive. The key to a successful drive, and what separates a drive from random fund-raising, is the planning that goes into it. The word "drive" connotates action, movement forward. If you set your goal, if you plan your attack, if you follow through with your fund-raising work, you will have a successful "drive."

A drive can be any type of fund-raising project in which the effort is carried out over a specified period of time. Drives include direct-mail campaigns, door-to-door candy sales, and membership solicitations.

What You Get

A Grant

A formal award of funds usually coming from a company or a foundation in response to a proposal. A significant motivation that prompts this charitable act is the IRS deduction that comes with it.

Grants come in a variety of packages, including:

GENERAL SUPPORT/UNRESTRICTED GRANT

These are the most liberal form of grants, as they allow the recipient to decide where to use the awarded monies within his organization, including putting them into the general operating budget if desired.

RESTRICTED GRANT

In awarding this type of grant, the funding organization stipulates how the money must be spent, i.e., to put on a roof, to cover postage costs. The grant has a very specific, limited purpose.

CHALLENGE GRANT

Many government programs and several large corporations give grants that require a "match" by the recipient. The simplest kind of match is the "I'll give you a dollar [or two or three] for every dollar you raise." Another type of match occurs when the donor offers your organization a grant of a specific amount of money with the stipulation that your organization raise an equal amount to match this grant within a period of time specified by the donor. In this way the donor challenges you to make the most of your fund-raising capabilities. This challenge grant becomes a leadership grant. Use of a leadership gift can be very effective here for the fund-raiser to leverage more support.

CONDITIONAL GRANT

Similar to a restricted grant, this type of grant requires the recipient to use the awarded funds for some predetermined purpose but allows the recipient more leeway in how it goes about fulfilling that purpose, i.e., the money may be for hiring a publicity director, but the grantee is allowed to choose that person. The conditions of this grant are set by the funding source and agreed to by the organization receiving the grant.

FUNDING CRISIS GRANTS

These monies are doled out to assist organizations suffering unexpected or temporary financial problems and come under a variety of headings, including:

Cash Reserve

Money to help cover your cash flow problems. (Don't know what cash flow problems are yet? Wait till you get your nonprofit organization started, i.e., when money has been promised but hasn't arrived yet and you've got bills to pay.)

Debt Reduction

If you have a deficit, this money goes to help reduce that deficit.

Emergency

Your roof caved in. Your food bank was robbed of all supplies. Your animal shelter needs a new heating system to pass inspection. . . .

Earmarked

Donors receive tax benefits only when the donation is made to an organization which has nonprofit status. These grants help new organizations that have applied for 501(c) (3) tax-exempt status (without which you cannot accept grant monies) but have not yet received it. Funding is issued to an organization that already has official nonprofit status who acts as a conduit to the organization awaiting that status, turning these monies over to that organization. In this way contribution requirements are met by the grantor and the new grantee is thereby able to benefit from this type of funding.

(For example, Punk and Judy, a newly organized puppet group still awaiting their nonprofit status, received a check for $2,000 from Merry Musicals, a twenty-two-year-old nonprofit theater company. XYZ Corporation had previously written a check to Merry Musicals for this $2,000 with the understanding that Merry Musicals would give this money to Punk and Judy.)

A Contribution or a Donation

Because it involves no forms to fill out, a less formal type of giving than a grant, these monies, goods, or services come from individuals or organizations in response to a drive in most instances.

Pledge

Whether you call it a donation, contribution, gift, or grant, it is the aim of the fund-raiser to bring the money into the organization. Not always do you get the money or the goods "up-front" or in-hand. Sometimes a prospective donor agrees to contribute to your organization but—for any number of reasons, i.e., to obtain the most advantageous tax deduction, to coincide with a stock market transaction—wishes to make the actual transaction at a future date.

While waiting for that date to collect this contribution, what you need to collect is a pledge. A pledge is quite simply a promise that someone or some organization is going to give your organization something. It is a formal statement that promises that a specified amount of funds or specific objects or services will be contributed by a specified date. When gathering pledges, it is best to try to get that pledge in writing with the amount and date clearly stated on a pledge form or card.

Sample Pledge Card

> Yes, I want to help find a home for all of Centerville's Fidos and Fifis.
>
> I pledge to give $________ to the Centerville Humane Society by ____________.
> (date)
>
> Sincerely,
>
> ____________ ____________
> (signature) (today's date)
>
> Name:________________________
> Address:______________________
> Phone:_______________________

Less formal than a pledge is a *commitment*. Generally, commitments are verbal, although sometimes they will come in the form of a letter. Usually, commitments do not specify a particular dollar figure or set a date for its contribution. Commitments can be helpful to raise spirits when a drive is foundering. They also can sometimes be used as a fund-raising tool, i.e., "I have a commitment from XYZ if I can get a commitment from you to match it."

Whenever possible, though, try to have a loose commitment made more formal by getting it in writing on a pledge card that is signed.

Leadership Gift

A good way to kick off a drive is to get a first gift. This gets the "bandwagon" effect started. The leadership gift can also often cover the basic administrative costs, such as postage, printing, food for volunteers, and so on. More than one fund-raising drive has never gotten off the ground because of the lack of a leadership gift.

A major leadership gift that the media will pick up on is extremely helpful, as it will serve to make other people aware of your drive and prompt them to give.

> The Florence J. Gould Foundation has donated $1 million to the French Institute/Alliance Française toward the construction of a 400-seat concert hall and performance space under its building at 22 East 60th Street.
>
> The grant represents the first major gift to a $4 million capital campaign undertaken by the institute to complete the expansion and renovation of its facilities. Robert Goelet, the president of the institute, called the gift "a major impetus" to the fund-raising drive.
>
> —*The New York Times,* March 18, 1986

With every drive we do, we should look for one or two "major impetus" gifts that can get P.R. for us. The president of the organization, the chairperson of the drive, or some other community leader is the ideal candidate to approach for this psychologically symbolic and fundamentally important first gift.

In-kind Donations

This type of gift to your organization does not come in the form of money but in goods and services. If you need a word processor to prepare your publicity materials effectively but don't have the $1,500 to buy one, consider approaching a local business about using their machines at night or on weekends. Another company may not be in a position to supply you with funds but may be more than happy to supply you with the desks, chairs and file cabinets you need which they have in storage. Other organizations will stuff, stamp, and mail out invitations to your upcoming benefit or advertise it free of charge in their newsletter.

Although no money changes hands, in-kind donations are

very important to your overall fund-raising plan. You get the goods, and the donor gets the tax deduction, just as if he had contributed the money the goods cost. A good budget incorporates potential in-kind gifts that have value for your needs and are equally strong evidence of your organization's fund-raising abilities.

APPENDIX B

Foundations

A foundation is a tax-exempt organization created to distribute funds to nonprofit organizations that have been earned as interest on the investment of their original endowment. Individuals or corporations set up foundations in order to take advantage of the maximum tax deduction allowed by the Internal Revenue Service. Very often, foundations are the first private supporters to recognize the worth of a new idea or project.

There are 24,000 grant-making foundations, divided into three basic types—family (the oldest), corporate, and community (the newest).

Family Foundations

For the most part, family foundations are established to honor the memory of a deceased person, but they are sometimes set up to shelter a certain amount of income belonging to a living person or persons. These are the most private of the "private" foundations, as the board of directors usually consists of family members or friends of the family. What the foundation will support customarily reflects the interests of the person the foundation is named after.

As an example, there is a wonderful small- to medium-sized family foundation in St. Paul, Minnesota, the Jerome

Foundation, set up by the family of the late Jerome Hill with money inherited from his grandfather, James J. Hill, a railroad and lumber magnate. Jerome was an exciting experimental filmmaker and artist in the twenties and thirties. The foundation's board of trustees still includes two of his sisters. The Jerome Foundation gives mostly to film and arts projects that Jerome Hill might have been interested in were he alive today. And because St. Paul and New York were his favorite American cities, over 95 percent of the foundation's grants are given to organizations in either Minnesota or New York.

Today, most family foundations have grown to large proportions (Ford, Rockefeller), and they bring in experts from all over the world to help with decisions on distributing their monies.

Corporate Foundations

By law, a corporation may take a deduction on up to 5 percent of its pre-tax profits that it donates to non-profit organizations. Usually, when a corporation reaches sizable proportions, it finds it useful to separate its fund-raising support activities from its business activities.

Most companies with an annual budget over $10 million have someone or even a group of people who handle small donations to nonprofit organizations. As corporate budgets get into the billion-dollar range, there are entire departments devoted solely to giving away corporate funds. The final step for a company truly interested in philanthropy over a long period of time is the establishment of a corporate foundation, which, by law, is separate from the interests of the mother company. It has a board of trustees that is different from the company's board but will usually be responsive to causes that are of interest to the company.

Community Foundations

Although only 225 of the 23,770 foundations in existence in this country in 1985 were community foundations, they are rapidly becoming very important for fund-raisers throughout most of the U.S. Generally, community foundations are set up to act as umbrellas for smaller family or corporate foundations or even individuals. As few as three and as many as several hundred funding sources can make up a community foundation pool. Their staff members usually have sophisticated project research capabilities, and their trustees are local corporate, religious, political, and educational leaders.

Created to serve the needs and interests of the communities in which they are located, these foundations are most responsive to new ideas that will in some way enhance life in their communities, and they also tend to like being involved in challenge grants.

Receiving a first-time grant from a community foundation is almost like getting the Good Housekeeping Seal of Approval and is very useful in establishing credibility for your other fund-raising efforts.

Foundations are as American as apple pie and just as idiosyncratic. And what is the foundation world like in the age of the new fund-raising? Changes in the way foundations approach problems, their structure, and their style of operations create an interesting, and often quirky, funding arena. Here are a few examples:

The Mukti Fund

With start-up assets of only $5,000, the Mukti (Sanskrit for "liberation") has given away $15,000 since its 1983 inception. Run by only two people who are committed to improving the quality of life through community projects,

Mukti may be the youngest and smallest American foundation with an international perspective.

National Flag Foundation

Based in Pittsburgh, this group's sole mission is to glorify the Stars and Stripes. Dedicated to running the American flag up flagpoles and encouraging everyone to salute it or at least respect it, the foundation has distributed over two million pamphlets on flag etiquette.

T. J. Martell Foundation for Leukemia and Cancer Research

Due to the tragic, untimely death of his twenty-one-year-old son to leukemia, Tony Martell, with the help of fellow record company executives, formed this foundation which has raised $15 million over the past decade for cancer research.

De Rance Foundation

Begun in 1946 with inherited interest from the Miller Brewing Company, the foundation was run by a married couple devoted to the Roman Catholic Church. They funded everything from leper colonies in Africa to antipoverty programs in Milwaukee. Once the world's largest Catholic charity, the De Rance Foundation is now embroiled in legal battles, as the couple who ran it split up.

The Joseph S. and Caroline Gruss Life Monument Fund

Announcing The Joseph S. and Caroline Gruss Life Monument Fund for Interest-Free Loans for the Construction and Expansion of Yeshivot and Day Schools

In recognition of the growth of enrollment in Jewish day schools and yeshivot in the New York Metropolitan area, and to help these schools to efficiently provide for expansion of their facilities, Mr. Joseph S. and Caroline Gruss announce the establishment of an interest-free loan fund to assist in the construction of yeshivot and day schools.

The Fund has been established under the auspices of the Federation of Jewish Philanthropies of New York under the following guidelines:

- Schools must meet criteria required to receive grants from the Fund for Jewish Education.
- Loans are available in amounts of up to $500,000. Schools must match the amount of the loan through a first mortgage issued by a bank or other financial lending institution.
- Co-signers are required to guarantee the amount of the interest-free loan.
- Repayment can be made over a period of up to 10 years.
- The Fund's Policy and Awards Committee will determine approval of all grants.

Applications should be submitted to the Hebrew Free Loan Society, Administrator of the Fund, 205 East 42nd Street, New York, N.Y. 10017, (212) 687-0188. The Hebrew Free Loan Society is supported by Federation.

FEDERATION

צדקה

FEDERATION OF JEWISH PHILANTHROPIES
130 EAST 59TH STREET • NEW YORK, NY 10022

Here's a fund that bought a half-page ad in *The New York Times* to get the word out on what they want to spend their money on and how they want to do it. It's a good example of why you should be continually on the lookout for information about foundations and fund-raising.

Stern Fund

Founders Edith and Edgar Stern did not want their fund to spend money perpetuating itself and so planned its ending at its beginning in 1936. In 1986 the fund divided up its last $325,000 among eight groups with missions as diverse as encouraging banks to invest in inner-city neighborhoods to aiding farm families to studying South Africa. The fund then threw a party to celebrate its demise.

* * *

Foundations hold a promise that corporations and individuals cannot. As reported in the July 1985 John O'Donnell Foundation *Newsletter,* "Many corporations have reacted to public pressure by increasing the number of grants they make while reducing the size of each grant." The amount of most foundation gifts is significantly greater than those awarded by corporations.

In addition, corporations and individuals have the sense that whatever foundations fund must be the cream of the crop—the best and the most promising organizations in their field. A foundation grant adds to your organization's credibility and can be useful in applying for other types of funds. (Most foundations are notoriously shy about having their name too prominently involved in a new group's efforts, however. Be sure to check with the foundation before putting out a press release or general announcement about their grant.)

If your group is not yet large enough, old enough, or proven enough to approach a private foundation, it probably will be someday. There are many very good books on the subject of foundation fund-raising. Suffice it to say that the elements of a good individual appeal are also the basis of a more sophisticated foundation proposal. You've already learned how to make an individual appeal. That knowledge, combined with information that can be found in your public library, can get you started raising money from foundations.

Grateful acknowledgment is made for permission to use the following works:

Cartoon by Tom Meyer. Copyright 1986 Tom Meyer.

"Giving a Big Hand," a chart from *Time* Magazine. Copyright © 1986 by Time Inc. By permission.

"Hard Times for Charity" by Brian O'Connell, excerpts from "The Hilton Will in Court" by M. Chambers, "The Iacocca Touch" by William E. Geist, and "New Allies: Credit Cards and Causes" by Andrew L. Yarrow, all from *The New York Times*. Copyright © 1986, 1987 by The New York Times Company. Reprinted by permission.

Cartoon by Roger Roth. Courtesy of the artist.

Checklist from Mellon Bank's booklet *Discover Total Resources*. © 1985 by Mellon Bank Corporation.

"Such stuff as dreams are made on . . . " from Raffle '86, a fund-raising project to benefit The New York Public Library. By permission of the Friends of the Library.

"How to contribute your money" membership application from The Second Stage. Courtesy of The Second Stage, New York, New York.

Excerpt from "Corporate America, Business Support of Cultural Institutions," *Natural History Magazine*, May 1986.

Membership application for Symphony Space. Copyright 1986 Isaiah Sheffer.

NBC corporate giving guildelines. All rights reserved, 1987, NBC Corporate Contributions.

Cartoon by Doug Marlette. Courtesy of Tribune Media Services.

Cartoon by C. Barsotti. Copyright 1986, USA Today. Reprinted with permission.

Letter from Oxfam America. By permission of Oxfam America.

List of donors from *The Numismatist*, July 1986. Reprinted through the courtesy of *The Numismatist*, the official publication of the American Numismatic Association, Colorado Springs, CO.

Advertisement for the Joseph S. and Caroline Gruss Life Monument Fund for Interest-Free Loans. By permission of the Federation of Jewish Philanthropies.

[illegible]

[illegible] copyright [illegible]

[illegible] by permission.

[illegible]

[illegible] by permission [illegible].

[illegible]

[illegible] Company.

[illegible]

[illegible] New York [illegible]

[illegible]

[illegible]

[illegible] Harcourt [illegible]

[illegible] permission.

[illegible]

[illegible]

[illegible]